GLOBAL PERSPECTIVES FOR EDUCATORS

Carlos F. Diaz
Florida Atlantic University

Byron G. Massialas
Florida State University

John A. Xanthopoulos
Palm Beach Community College

Allyn and Bacon
Boston • London • Toronto • Sydney • Tokyo • Singapore

Series Editor: Frances Helland
Series Editorial Assistant: Bridget Keane
Director of Education Programs: Ellen Mann Dolberg
Marketing Manager: Brad Parkins
Production Editor: Christopher H. Rawlings
Editorial-Production Service: Omegatype Typography, Inc.
Composition and Prepress Buyer: Linda Cox
Manufacturing Buyer: Suzanne Lareau
Cover Administrator: Jennifer Hart
Electronic Composition: Omegatype Typography, Inc.

Library of Congress Cataloging-in-Publication Data

Diaz, Carlos (Carlos F.)
    Global perspectives for educators / by Carlos F. Diaz, Byron G.
Massialas, John A. Xanthopoulos.
        p.   cm.
    Includes bibliographical references and index.
    ISBN 0-205-26366-6
    1. International education—United States.   2. Multicultural
education—United States.   3. Pluralism (Social Sciences)—Study and
teaching—United States.   4. Education, Humanistic—United States.
I. Massialas, Byron G.   II. Xanthopoulos, John.
III. Title.
LC1090.D53 1998
370.116—dc21   98-20918
                                                                            CIP

Printed in the United States of America
10 9 8 7 6 5 4 3 2   03 02 01 00 99

*We would like to dedicate this book
to all of the children of the world.*

Contents

Preface

With the arrival of the twenty-first century and the new millennium, educators, parents, and ordinary citizens are increasingly realizing that they need the tools to meet the demands of a new era. Modern technology has contributed to the shrinking of the world; it has, indeed, expedited the process of globalization. What are the consequences of this process on individuals or groups of individuals? How does one cope with a transition from living in a local community with provincial perspectives to living in a world community with cosmopolitan perspectives? How do we educate children and young people to be full-fledged members of the New World environment and respond effectively to the promises and challenges of this new reality?

Global education provides a means to respond to the challenges and the promises of the new era. In general, it seeks to offer to students a different perspective—a global perspective—in which to study and work. If global education in the classroom is effective, one result will be the development of a sense of global efficacy among students—that is, an understanding of how the world system operates and the feeling that they are capable of influencing it. As students examine world issues, they learn that in a world of cosmopolitans there is hardly any place for provincials.

This text accomplishes the following goals:

- To clarify the concept of global education and to describe its relationship with other fields, such as multicultural education and social studies

- To offer teachers and prospective teachers a framework for studying world affairs
- To provide examples of a global education curriculum and related activities for students
- To propose ways that educational objectives for global education can be created clearly and be placed under established categories of learning and instruction for which the school is responsible
- To point out ways in which objectives for global studies connect with the curriculum, springboard materials, instructional strategies, and assessment procedures
- To offer a selection of global issues in some depth—human rights, the bioenvironment, population change, global security—information that provides the background material on these issues for classroom use.

There are two primary audiences for this text. The first audience is composed of prospective teachers studying in teacher preparation programs. This book is an excellent foundation for the global education component of teacher preparation. The second audience consists of practicing teachers who want to broaden their backgrounds on global issues.

In the spirit of inquiry teaching and learning, this book is not offered as a definitive treatise on global education. Rather, it is offered as a springboard for discussion by the profession. We believe the book will generate interest in the field; criticism and debate both inside and outside of the classroom; and provide educators with a solid background in the main issues of global education.

Acknowledgments

The authors would like to thank several individuals who have helped with the preparation of this book. Victoria Samaras Polentas provided invaluable assistance in the preparation of Chapters 4, 5, and 6 which concern global issues.

The authors are also very grateful to Marcella Centola for her assistance in arranging the format of the chapters in this text. We would like to recognize the assistance of Virginia Lanigan in conceptualizing this project. We would also like to thank Frances Helland for her patience, professionalism, and suggestions during the development of this manuscript. Also, we would like to thank everyone who reviewed the manuscript: M. Eugene Gilliom, The Ohio State University; Xue Lan Rong, University of North Carolina at Chapel Hill; Joan Thrower Timm, University of Wisconsin–Oshkosh; and Dr. Wayne L. Wolf, South Suburban College.

Finally, we would like to thank Diane Diaz and Eva Xanthopoulos, for their lifelong encouragement and support.

C.F.D.

B.G.M.

J.A.X.

1

GLOBAL AND MULTICULTURAL EDUCATION: PARTNERS IN PLURALISTIC TEACHING

Major Points

- Global and multicultural education, while generally distinct, have some areas of overlap, such as human rights. Multicultural education serves as both a foundation and a complement to global education.

- Traditional educational practices have de-emphasized multicultural and global perspectives.

- The cultural identification of teachers is very significant in establishing a comfortable academic climate in which global education can take place.

- Secondary teachers are generally more supportive of global perspectives in the curriculum than their elementary counterparts.

- Teachers of multicultural and global education should incorporate both mainstream and transformative academic knowledge in their lessons.

- Research indicates that students who have been exposed to controversial issues in an open classroom setting develop stronger feelings of citizen duty and positive global attitudes.

- Stressing global perspectives in the curriculum does not inhibit pride in one's own nation.

- Many leading academic organizations in the United States have supported the incorporation of global education within the curriculum, and many states have required or promoted the inclusion of global perspectives in teaching.

- The growing international nature of the economy of the United States requires that students be prepared to work in positions that require global literacy and sophistication.

- The lack of national global literacy can have significant negative effects in economic, cultural, and political matters.

A few years ago, one of the authors was asked to deliver a keynote lecture for a teacher workshop in a school district in the Western United States. After the lecture, the host asked him if he would like to visit the multicultural fair being held at a local elementary school. He indicated that he would and expected to view exhibits on the ethnic diversity and history of that community. He also expected to see exhibits about different cultural groups that contributed to the development of that state, region, or perhaps the United States.

Upon his arrival, he was taken to the gymnasium where the multicultural fair was taking place. He saw a series of booths on the perimeter of the gymnasium. Each booth celebrated a different country, but no booth explained cultural and ethnic diversity in that community, state, or of the United States.

This brief anecdote illustrates that there is significant confusion over the definition of *multicultural* and what constitutes multicultural education. The principal at the multicultural fair did not distinguish conceptually between national and international notions of culture. The fair was actually quite extensive and the exhibits well presented, but the event more accurately should have been called an international fair or "Understanding the Global Village."

The purpose of this chapter is not to provide specific global education content or pedagogical features (those are provided in later chapters), but to explore whether global education should be viewed as a curricular necessity or luxury. As the twenty-first century begins, many people do not view global literacy as an indispensable academic objective for all students in the United States.

DEFINING MULTICULTURAL
AND GLOBAL EDUCATION

To avoid the confusion that occurred at the school fair, one must define the parameters of multicultural and global education. The two fields have many areas of overlap, including the study of cultural diversity, human rights, varied curricular perspectives, and prejudice reduction (see Figure 1.1). The fields vary most significantly in the context surrounding them.

Multicultural education frames the above-mentioned topics within the context of the nation in which the student resides. Global education examines these topics in countries other than the student's nation of residence. Global education typically uses references to the student's nation of residence in the form of cross-national comparisons.

This fundamental conceptual distinction between multicultural and global education is critical because it is often blurred in the school curriculum and classroom practice. An elementary teacher in the United States who shares with students a story about Kwame, a young man in Ghana, is providing students with some basic content about West Africa. Therefore, this teacher is primarily practicing global, not multicultural education.

A high school history teacher in California discusses World War II, and then the students read various primary source accounts of Japanese Americans interned at the Manzanar Camp. In addition, the students read Franklin Roosevelt's Executive Order No. 9066 and

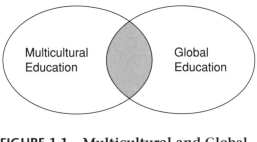

**FIGURE 1.1   Multicultural and Global
Education**

President Roosevelt's rationale for signing this order mandating internment of persons of Japanese extraction. They also read some accounts of top military officials responsible for carrying out the internment. Through these readings, the students examine multiple voices surrounding the internment. These varied and sometimes conflicting perspectives involve an issue set within the United States. This part of the curriculum is in the realm of multicultural education. It could later be used as a springboard for looking at human rights internationally, which would be global education.

While this text distinguishes multicultural content primarily as internal to a nation and global content as external to it, other definitions have been written that do not agree with this distinction. For example, Pamela and Iris Tiedt note,

> Defined more broadly, thus, multicultural education connects the study of other countries, the concept of the world as a global village, and recognition of the need for everyone on this planet to collaborate to insure clean air and conserve our resources. Focus on international studies brings an awareness of the shared concerns of nations around the world (Tiedt & Tiedt, 1995, p. 17).

Understanding diversity, at home and abroad, is a critical component of a well-rounded education. The inclusion of both multicultural and global education in school curriculum provides students with complementary approaches—each geared toward the understanding of diverse perspectives in national and international contexts. However, one approach does not substitute for the other.

Ideally, students in the United States should be exposed to curricula with significant levels of both multicultural and global education. In learning about other societies, students should be made aware of the diversity present in other nations' populations and how that diversity can affect national and international issues.

The story about Kwame in Ghana mentioned earlier does not provide an adequate substitute for curriculum aimed at teaching about African Americans. However, students receiving a basic understanding of West Africa would find this background useful when studying about African Americans.

The high school history class reading extensively about the internment of Japanese Americans during World War II still requires additional background to understand Japan–U.S. relations and today's Japanese society. Knowledge acquired about Japanese American culture and the stoicism demonstrated by Japanese Americans during their internment will be a valuable asset to those high school history students when they study contemporary Japanese society.

Clearly, there are links in the knowledge base and concepts necessary to implement multicultural and global education. Teachers must understand these links so they may, in turn, emphasize them to their students.

TRADITIONAL INFLUENCES ON MULTICULTURAL AND GLOBAL EDUCATION

Before engaging in a detailed analysis of multicultural and global education in the United States, it is useful for educators to understand why neither of these approaches has been part of traditional education. After all, traditional educational practices serve as the backdrop against which all changes in education are measured. Why have multicultural and global education not become integral parts of traditional education in the United States? According to Bennett (1995), "because schools are patterned after the predominant culture, it is essential to understand the macrocultural world view that originated primarily in Britain and Western Europe. This is not an easy task for those who happen to share this view of the world and take it for granted" (pp. 57–58).

Like beauty defined by the beholder, a dominant group in any society tends to create curriculum that places it and its nation as the hub of all knowledge. Thus, traditional education in the United States has tended to de-emphasize or ignore the role of nondominant groups in its society. Among these are ethnic minority groups, women, and working class persons. Similar curricular treatment in the international arena has been given to knowledge that emanates from Latin America, Africa, and Asia. The reasons for this historical pattern are not particularly perplexing. Those in the position to shape curriculum were doing so in their own rather homogeneous image. This historical pattern of education is not unique to the

United States. It may be found, to a significant degree, in traditional education provided by nations across the globe. One of the reasons for this traditional curricular focus is that the role and interests of the dominant group have been defined in the curriculum as synonymous with the national interest. The roles of smaller or weaker groups often have been regarded as secondary, even antithetical, to the national interest; the national interest was always viewed as good.

A curriculum with a significant multicultural and global education base also promotes a broad pedagogical approach. Routine analysis of curricular topics from multiple perspectives nurtures students' abilities to operate at the higher levels of Bloom's taxonomy of learning.

Nearly three decades ago, a high school student was taking a course entitled "Americanism versus Communism." The course was taught in all Florida high schools by a mandate of the state legislature. The text showed a chart comparing refrigerator production in the Soviet Union and the United States. The number of refrigerators in the United States far exceeded those in the Soviet Union. The teacher cited the discrepancy in refrigerator production as clear evidence of a superior system in the United States. The student asked, "Is this a fair comparison, since the Soviets don't place much emphasis on the production of consumer goods such as refrigerators?" The teacher dismissed the student's question as irrelevant, yet the student had raised a valid point, which needed to be considered in comparing the two societies.

This anecdote illustrates that teaching global issues and incorporating the perspectives of others, even if they are inimical to one's own perspective, raises the level of analysis and critical thinking in the classroom. Likewise, domestic topics taught from varied but germane perspectives often yield fascinating classroom dialogue. What this approach does not produce is a single dogmatic and perennial curricular belief.

Consider the typical unit on the American Revolution encountered by U.S. students at various grade levels. How much time is spent studying the views of colonists who wanted to remain loyal to England? Were the revolutionaries a significant majority of the colonial population or a determined minority? What was the fate of colonial loyalists once the new United States was born? Did freedom and independence apply to them as well as to the successful revolutionaries? What views were held by the British people about fighting to retain control of the American colonies? These questions, along with many others, should be explored in a topic presented as frequently in the school curriculum as the American Revolution is. Too often these questions are neither posed nor answered in presentations of the topic; instead, classes focus largely on the activities of the successful American revolutionaries.

A multicultural–global approach to teaching about the American Revolution would address those questions. It would also deal with why the British government considered the colonists' demands to be unreasonable. Furthermore, the American Revolution, which is often taught as an inevitable event, would be presented as a choice made by some American colonists. (British colonists in Canada chose not to revolt and eventually received their independence from Britain in stages.)

Teaching a more multicultural and global view of the American Revolution requires teachers to have a significant knowledge base that extends beyond the content of most textbooks. These additional perspectives, when presented in a scholarly and well-documented manner, add significantly to student interest and explain in much greater detail the dilemmas faced by those who fought on both sides of the American Revolution.

THE CULTURAL IDENTIFICATION
OF THE TEACHER

An essential element in the effective implementation of either multicultural or global education is the cultural identification of the teacher. Even when the curriculum presents topics from diverse perspectives, the teacher brings new material into focus and provides the background that gives perspective to new information.

James A. Banks has developed a typology to classify the cultural identity of individuals. The six stages of this typology are as follows:

1. **Ethnic Psychological Captivity** Persons internalize negative stereotypes about their own ethnic group and exhibit low self-esteem.
2. **Ethnic Encapsulation** Persons believe that ethnic separation is the best course for themselves and their group. Highly

ethnocentric behavior is common in this stage and so are suspicions of other ethnic groups and nationalities.

3. **Ethnic Identity Clarification**   Persons have developed self-acceptance and respond in a generally positive way to ethnic or cultural groups which are not their own. Persons generally cannot cope well with analysis of the shortcomings of their cultural group or nationality before having reached this stage.

4. **Biethnicity**   Persons are as equally comfortable operating in the culture of another ethnic or cultural group in their nation as they are in their own.

5. **Multiethnicity**   Persons are able to function in nonsuperficial ways in several ethnic cultures present in their nation.

6. **Globalism**   In addition to functioning well in several ethnic cultures in their nation, persons at this stage can also function well internationally. These persons have a balance of ethnic, national, and global commitments (Banks, 1994, pp. 224–227).

Ideally, teachers should all be stage 6 persons, in order to comfortably deliver multicultural and global content as well as to provide the proper affective climate for students. The teacher preparation curriculum should be responsible for creating significant numbers of teachers capable of functioning at the globalism stage.

In reviewing the findings of the National Council for Accreditation of Teacher Education (NCATE) regarding the incorporation of multicultural and global education in teacher preparation, Gollnick noted that the most common areas of weakness were the following:

- There is a lack of emphasis on studies or experiences related to culturally diverse populations; multicultural experiences are limited.
- The curriculum lacks adequate content and experiences in global and/or multicultural perspectives (Gollnick, 1992, p. 235).

These findings generate concern for educators who wish to see multicultural and global perspectives incorporated throughout the curriculum.

Other indicators of the cultural identification levels of teachers were found in a study designed to test the Banks typology. Ford (1979) analyzed over 500 teachers in Texas. She found that over 75% of teachers tested were below stage 3 (ethnic identity clarification). Very few teachers reached stage 5 (multiethnicity). At the time of the Ford study, stage 6 (globalism), had not yet been added to the Banks typology.

Despite these results, most teachers in the Ford study were practicing in culturally heterogeneous classrooms. The Gollnick and Ford findings suggest that teachers who can function well in cultures outside of their own and have a strong multicultural–global knowledge base are not very common in the United States. Developing significant numbers of teachers with this background will not occur unless it becomes a societal priority.

ATTITUDES TOWARD GLOBAL EDUCATION

Tucker surveyed teachers in Dade County (Miami, Florida). He found that 90% of teachers surveyed in grades 7–12 felt that global education should be an important part of the curriculum. However, only 42% felt that they were qualified to teach global education (Tucker, 1983). The findings, if they are representative of the larger universe of secondary teachers, suggest that the attitudinal predisposition toward global education is strong. The inclination simply needs to be reinforced with strong in-service programs in order to make global education more pervasive in secondary classrooms.

A contrasting result was found in another study, which surveyed elementary teachers. Herman (1983) found that only 20% of elementary teachers indicated that global education was important for students in grades 1–6. The discrepancies in attitudes toward global education found between the secondary teachers in the Tucker study and the elementary teachers in the Herman study are somewhat perplexing. Perhaps, since elementary social studies programs (where teachers need to assign the bulk of global curricula) focus on the family, community, region, and nation, global topics appear peripheral. Another possible reason for the discrepancy is that elementary educators may feel less qualified to teach global issues than their secondary counterparts. This, in turn, could affect their view of the necessity for global education in the elementary curriculum.

Knowing that the elementary years are an optimal time to teach about diversity on a global scale might sway the attitudes of the elementary educators surveyed by Herman. One study found that children 10 or younger were more receptive to learning about people in other nations. At age 14, the same children were less receptive, and the distinctions made about persons in other countries were based on personalities or political and religious behaviors that often had negative connotations (Evans, 1987, p. 548).

In summarizing the cultural identifications of educators and their attitudes toward multicultural and global education, a number of issues emerge. First, teachers and administrators with positive attitudes toward cultures that are not their own generally are going to be supportive toward both multicultural and global education. It would be a rare case if an educator supported global—but not multicultural—education, or the reverse. Educators, parents, or policy makers at the ethnic psychological captivity or ethnic encapsulation stages of the Banks typology are likely to oppose both multicultural and global education.

Another point influencing attitudes is the perception that multicultural and global education will detract from national unity in the United States and diminish national pride. This concern has not been substantiated by research. Furthermore, it is rooted in either/or logic often found in Western thought: "National unity must come only from the dilution and eventual extinction of minority cultural groups in a nation. You may not have all. You favor the (patriotic) national interest, *or* you support global interdependence; the two are not compatible."

These views are present in schools, communities, and government. Educators must recognize this and explain that neither multicultural nor global education, as defined by leading theorists, proposes a deterioration of national unity or pride. There is no reason why providing students with multicultural and global literacy should inhibit their developing and maintaining pride in their own nation. This point must be stressed in order to gain support for multicultural and global curricular change from educators and members of the community.

MAINSTREAM AND TRANSFORMATIVE KNOWLEDGE IN MULTICULTURAL EDUCATION

One of the reasons why multicultural education has generated supporters and detractors is that it seeks to broaden the nature of the content and perspectives presented in schools. Traditional teaching has emphasized only mainstream academic knowledge.

Banks has developed a useful typology of knowledge that defines mainstream academic knowledge and transformative academic knowledge. He describes mainstream academic knowledge as follows:

The concepts paradigms, theories, and explanations that constitute traditional Western-centric knowledge in history and the behavioral and social sciences. (Banks, 1994, p. 147)

In contrast, Banks defines transformative academic knowledge as the following:

The facts, concepts, paradigms, themes, and explanations that challenge mainstream academic knowledge and expand and substantially revise established canons, paradigms, theories, explanations, and research methods. When transformative academic paradigms replace mainstream ones, a scientific revolution has occurred. What is more normal is that transformative academic paradigms coexist with established ones. (Banks, 1994, p. 147)

The very nature of a multicultural curriculum dictates that students will be exposed to both mainstream and transformative academic knowledge. From the interplay of these two knowledge paradigms, students may gain a much richer understanding of the topic being studied.

Mainstream academic knowledge teaches that the settlement of the United States was largely an East-to-West process. This process accounts for nearly all immigrants who emigrated from Europe. A multicultural approach to the settlement of the United States would begin with the notion that North America was already settled before any Europeans arrived. Consequently, an area that is already inhabited cannot be "discovered," and its settlement was not simply an East-to-West process.

While recognizing that the bulk of settlers came from Europe and followed the East-to-West settlement pattern, transformative knowledge should be added to examine the Asian West-to-East settlement pattern and South-to-North path traveled by settlers emigrating from Mexico. The forced settlement of Africans in North America should be included, followed by an examination of the internal migrations of African Americans.

Many people in the United States who have learned mainstream academic knowledge in government and economics are under the impression that "there is a job in the United States for every person seeking one," but this is another example of how mainstream academic knowledge can be limiting. This conclusion suggests that independent of people's skills, the number of jobs exceeds the number of job seekers. Consequently, this view supports the notion that all unemployed U.S. adults simply do not want to work. While textbooks do not teach this belief explicitly, it is a widely held view inferred from the mainstream curriculum.

Economics students taking classes that incorporate multicultural–global perspectives and transformative knowledge would learn the following:

- The economy of the United States has never employed all adults seeking work at any time in history.
- Full employment in the U.S. economy is often defined as around 4½–5% unemployment.
- A small measure of unemployment is endemic in capitalist economics.
- Ascribed factors such as race, gender, ethnicity, and immigrant status significantly affect unemployment rates, even when skills are comparable.
- The great majority of funds in government transfer programs in the United States do not benefit the poor but target people who are middle-class or upper-class (Gollnick & Chinn, 1998, pp. 35–71).

This transformative economic knowledge could be researched and weighed against students' existing notions of the U.S. economy and government economic policy.

One of the side effects of presenting transformative knowledge as part of a multicultural approach to education is that students unfamiliar with the new information may view it as controversial. This transformative knowledge may be seen as controversial because it conflicts with previously taught beliefs, not because the transformative knowledge is incorrect. One should always carefully check the accuracy of all knowledge presented to students, but this is particularly true for transformative knowledge.

Students may initially resist accepting transformative knowledge. A suggested response to such students is, "If you doubt it, please research the topic yourself." If students take up that challenge, they will often realize that what at first seemed like an incongruous statement turns out to be true, once all of the pertinent information is learned.

Students who are taught transformative academic knowledge are bound to experience some academic dissonance as new paradigms are compared to traditional ones. The textbook remains the main source of school knowledge in the United States (Goodlad, 1984); this finding suggests that by largely using textbook material, controversy and transformative knowledge in the classroom are reduced. While the reduction of controversial topics may seem safer for some teachers, is it really the best for students? Soley notes the following research findings relating the study of controversial issues to student achievement and behavior:

- Positive citizenship outcomes were correlated with students' opportunities to study controversial issues in a supportive classroom atmosphere.
- Social studies classes devoid of controversial issues had little or no effect on students' political interest or participation.
- Students exposed to larger numbers of controversial issues had higher levels of citizen duty, political participation, and efficacy.
- Students who recalled a wider range of views discussed in their classrooms were more trusting in society, more politically confident and interested, as well as more socially integrated.
- Students' perceptions of an open classroom atmosphere were positively correlated with positive global attitudes.
- Students who participated in classes where they initiated more of the discussion were more likely to feel that people can successfully affect their political system (Soley, 1996, pp. 9–10).

In spite of these findings, many educators treat transformative knowledge and controversial issues with trepidation. While depending on the textbook may minimize discussions of transformative or controversial information, this approach is responsible for much student criticism claiming that the curriculum is dull, pedantic, and boring. Certainly, entertainment value cannot be the major criterion for curriculum building; however, a multicultural–global approach to curriculum, which includes significant amounts of transformative knowledge and the discussion of controversial issues, is not only more interesting to students, but quite academically defensible.

MAINSTREAM AND TRANSFORMATIVE KNOWLEDGE IN GLOBAL EDUCATION

Mainstream and transformative knowledge, defined in the preceding section, in some ways apply differently to global and multicultural education. Global issues and information can be, and often are, presented to students using only the mainstream knowledge paradigms. One example of this might be looking at the histories of other nations only when their histories intersect with the history of the United States. Since mainstream academic knowledge represents the bulk of school knowledge, students in the United States are much more familiar with Commodore Perry opening Japan to Western trade than they are with the Meiji Restoration in Japanese history. Similarly, U.S. students are better acquainted with the military government of Japan during World War II than they are with democratic Japanese governments in the past three decades. These patterns of knowledge repeat themselves with other nations as well. Often, the intersection of another nation's history with the history of the United States serves as the major criterion for curricular emphasis. Dorman calls for an end to "cultural narcissism" in teaching global issues (Dorman, 1992, p. 3). He also calls for an effort to "denationalize the curriculum" and shift from an emphasis on nationalism and "number oneness" to one that stresses global interdependence. Dorman further states that he does not see why teaching students to become world citizens should inhibit their developing pride in their own country (Dorman, 1992, p. 7).

Another example of mainstream academic knowledge is when students are taught world issues from bipolar perspectives, such as in the interest of the United States and its allies or the former Soviet Union and its allies. With the dissolution of the Soviet Union into independent republics, this approach is used considerably less today but its effects still linger. For example, was U.S. involvement in the Vietnam War a classic struggle between communists and democrats for ideological superiority, or was it the final phase of a decades-old struggle by the Vietnamese to end outside control in their nation and reunify the country?

In order to attempt to answer this question, some transformative knowledge is useful. The United States sided with the South Vietnamese government in opposing national elections in 1956 aimed at reunifying the nation. These elections had been part of the agreement that partitioned Vietnam into North and South. However, the South Vietnamese and U.S. governments were concerned that Ho Chi Minh, leader of communist North Vietnam, would win the elections in 1956. These elections were never held. The United States opposed the democratic process in 1956, but ostensibly fought to preserve it a decade later. Students of global issues should be provided with this information and then guided through a scholarly discussion on why the United States became involved in Vietnam.

Another issue of concern involving mainstream and transformative knowledge in global education is the distressing performance of U.S. students in tests of geographical literacy. One study asked students from the United States, the former Soviet Union, and seven other nations to identify 16 places on a world map. Students from the United States came in last place (Grosvenor, 1989). The argument that U.S. students need to know the basics about the world and its people has considerable merit. However, knowing that Bogotá is the capital of Colombia or that Colombia is a leading exporter of coffee does not give students much insight into the complex political dynamics of that nation. The regional geography approach to global issues can result in an "if it is Tuesday, it must be Belgium" response by students. Basic concepts and mainstream academic knowledge about the world are valuable. However, they must be supplemented with transformative academic information such as the following facts:

- Canada, not Japan, is the leading trading partner of the United States.
- Most people in the world who speak English, speak it as a second language.
- The most populous Muslim nation in the world is not an Arab country. It is Indonesia.

- The success of the Haitian Revolution prompted Napoleon to sell the Louisiana Purchase to the United States rather than to defend it.
- The nation of Panama was created out of a province of Colombia with direct military assistance from the United States.
- U.S., British, and French troops were sent to intervene in internal civil conflicts in Russia after World War I.

These are but a few examples of transformative knowledge. Because they are frequently not included or stressed in the mainstream curriculum, they often startle students when first encountered. That temporary bewilderment underscores the power of transformative academic knowledge; it suggests to students that they need to be receptive to "rearranging the furniture of the mind."

INSTITUTIONALIZATION OF MULTICULTURAL AND GLOBAL EDUCATION

It was noted earlier in this chapter that multicultural and global education are both in their relative infancy as part of the daily practice of education in the United States. When multicultural education is currently practiced, most of the activities fall into the "heroes and holidays" category. The underlying mainstream curriculum remains unreconstructed. Textbooks are more pluralistic today than they were two or three decades ago. Still, they dominate too much of the curriculum and generally contain too little transformative academic knowledge.

Teaching about Harriet Tubman and Dr. Martin Luther King, Jr. during February (Black History Month) will not raise any eyebrows in most schools. Yet, most Americans do not know that Dr. Carter G. Woodson was the originator of Negro History Week; Black History Week preceded Black History Month. Dr. Woodson hoped for a time when African American content would be interwoven in all school subjects, so there would be no need to call attention to Black History with a special week or month. Seven decades after the advent of Negro History Week in 1926, Black History Month is still with us and the incorporation of African American content into the mainstream curriculum proceeds at a slow pace.

In order to promote the institutionalization of multicultural and global education, one should examine the five common goals of the two fields, developed by Cole:

1. To promote student understanding of social living in groups.
2. To aid in understanding of "the other," especially ethnic and foreign cultural appreciation.
3. To foster the understanding of interrelatedness and interdependence.
4. To assist in the development of skills in living with diversity.
5. To assist in the adjustment to changes for the future (Cole, 1984, p. 153).

These goals are consensus oriented and likely to be supported in many communities. However, some educators and schools will respond to the incorporation of multicultural and global curricula by pointing out that they held a multicultural food fest or are teaching regional geography of the world and thus, "We are already doing it."

In comparing multicultural and global education, Kobus suggests that both fields focus on the analysis of equity (Kobus, 1992, p. 225). Multicultural education stresses national equity while global education stresses international equity. Authors such as Alexandre (1989) and O'Brien and Sreberny-Mohammadi (1993) have proposed that no version of global education is complete without a thorough discussion of gender issues in the international arena. Any discussion of gender issues, whether at the national or global level, involves a thorough analysis of the concept of equity. There are certainly forces in every society that would prefer the curriculum not to focus on equity issues. Educators who promote multicultural and global education must contend with this while continuing to stress that schools in the United States must not simply be mirrors of Main Street, but also windows to the world.

Fain raises and then answers the question, "Shouldn't elementary schools be concentrating on patriotism instead of global concerns?" To this question, which is predicated on either/or logic, Fain responds that global education is not a thinly disguised attempt to sell some vague form of "one-worldism" or "world citizenship." It is an effort to add a global dimension to a solid background of local, state, and national citizenship (Fain, 1988, p. 28). Essentially, Fain is saying to the critics of global education that this field does not attempt to usurp patriotism; rather, it represents a "patriotism plus" understanding of other cultures and global interdependence. This position should assuage at least some of the concerns about global education de-emphasizing patriotism.

Diaz has identified other concerns that could prevent the implementation of multicultural education. Among these are the following:

- Multicultural education is a curricular fad that will disappear if educators simply wait.
- A multicultural curriculum is attempting to force particular conclusions on students.
- Multicultural education politicizes the curriculum. (This assumes the total absence of a political dimension in the traditional curriculum.)
- Multicultural education is restructuring the canon of knowledge.
- Communities may not beleive multicultural education to be correlated with higher standardized test scores.
- Educators may feel ill equipped to implement multicultural education (Diaz, 1992, pp. 193–202).

The potential elements of resistance to multicultural education raised by Diaz could also apply to efforts to implement global education. Educators should note that effective instruction in global education is predicated on having a broad understanding of cultural diversity in one's own nation. For example, if students do not understand Mexican Americans who live in their communities and schooling has not promoted an academic understanding of these people, it is highly unlikely that students will understand Mexican culture and institutions in Mexico. In essence, multicultural education serves both as a foundation and a complement to global education.

INFLUENCES ON GLOBAL EDUCATION

Since global education has not been a very significant component of traditional education in the United States, educators must understand the reasons. More importantly, they must understand the contemporary forces that create a need for students in the United States to have an education that is global in nature. A number of influences on American education strongly suggest that global education should move from the margins to the core of the curriculum.

Planning and implementing curriculum is somewhat like launching a planetary space probe. One must aim not at where the planet is, but at where it will be when the probe arrives. Astronomers have the advantage of working with predictable orbits. Educators must plan curricula to prepare students for a future that is somewhat unknown.

Academic Organizations and Global Education

One of the leading advocates of global education in the United States is the National Council for the Social Studies (NCSS). This organization adopted a position statement on global education that stated the following:

1. People are constantly being affected by transnational, cross-cultural, and multicultural influences.
2. There are a variety of actors (states, multinational corporations, private voluntary associations, and individuals) on the world stage.
3. The fate of humanity cannot be separated from the state of the world environment.
4. There are linkages between social, political, and ecological realities and alternative futures.
5. Citizen participation is critical in both local and world affairs (NCSS, 1982, pp. 37–38).

These goals by the nation's leading organization of social studies educators indicate that a curriculum that results in graduates with provincial understanding is no longer acceptable. A problem in implementing these goals is encountered when, according to the American Association of Colleges of Teacher Education, it is estimated that only about 5% of the nation's elementary and secondary teachers have had academic preparation in the international topics or issues (Council on Learning, 1981). Clearly, teacher education programs are going to have to increase their emphasis on international topics if global education is to become pervasive in the classrooms of the United States.

The National Commission on Social Studies in the Schools issued a report that combined citizenship education and global education. This commission, composed of members of three major organizations of historians and social studies educators, emphasized the teaching of history in a global context. The report states, "The special experience of the United States must be set in the context of world affairs, so our continuing involvement with other nations will be seen as normal and inescapable" (National Commission on Social Studies in the Schools, 1989, p. 14).

Integrating historical, cultural, political, and economic events that occurred in the United States with similar events that occurred internationally gives this knowledge a much richer texture. Students making connections between related national and international topics are operating at a higher cognitive level than those merely remembering facts.

While global education is frequently perceived as being wholly in the area of the social studies, it also has a significant dimension in science. The American Association for the Advancement of Science (1989, p. 23) has called for the teaching of science in a global context. The sciences are truly international disciplines, and their presentation in the elementary and secondary classrooms of the United States should reflect this. The scientific method calls for a uniform standard wherever science is practiced. This might give some the impression that science does not vary anywhere in the world. However, how societies choose to invest their money in scientific research is very much a societal decision based on a given society's values. Switzerland has many world-class physicists, but it would be unlikely for those physicists to devote their talents to producing *Star Wars* lasers to fashion a nuclear umbrella. Philosophical and ethical issues surrounding science and scientific applications also have global consequences. Study of these issues should be as routine in science classrooms as finding a periodic chart of elements in a chemistry laboratory.

Another change slowly occurring in the academic arena is in teacher preparation. Of the 1,200 colleges and universities that prepare teachers in the United States, 514 are accredited by the National Council for Accreditation of Teacher Education (NCATE). This organization requires colleges of education to document an emphasis on cultural diversity in the curriculum and fieldwork performed by prospective teachers (Gollnick, 1992, pp. 226–227). In addition, the American Association of Colleges for Teacher Education (AACTE) has adopted a resolution supporting global education in the teacher preparation curriculum (Gollnick, 1992, p. 225).

If prestigious academic organizations and groups of scholars have adopted strong statements of support for global education, why isn't global education more pervasive in today's schools? Part of the answer is due to the United States not having a national system of education. A myriad of local and state authorities control the nation's schools, colleges, and universities. No one has the power to institute national comprehensive change in curriculum or teacher preparation. State and local authorities can choose to incorporate position statements of learned societies and academic organizations, or they may choose to ignore them. The impetus to provide a more global education for U.S. students is there, but it currently is resulting in a slow, evolutionary change.

State and Local Influences on Global Education

You may have seen the bumper sticker on automobiles that states, "Think Globally, Act Locally." This brief phrase captures the link between individual communities and the world. Energy consumption patterns in individual U.S. communities, when added together, determine whether the United States is an energy-importing or an energy-exporting nation. The United States exported energy until the early 1960s. Since that time, it has imported energy. A country which imports energy cannot afford to have its external sources of energy curtailed. Consequently, energy use, which occurs at the local level, provides a striking example of a local decision with international implications.

Another local issue with global connections is economic development. Historically, isolationist tendencies in the United States were supported by the fact that the U.S. was its own best customer. Today, slightly over 25% of the gross national product of the United States is dependent on international trade. Cities like Smyrna, Tennessee, and Marysville, Ohio, are respectively sites for Nissan and Honda automobile manufacturing plants. While these communities may not have had a traditional link with Japan, they do now. Greenville, South Carolina, has been successful in convincing a number of companies chartered outside the United States to open plants in that community. These examples illustrate that the line between local and global issues is blurred when it comes to economics.

At the state level, there have also been some initiatives to support global education. Merryfield (1991, p. 11) cites a survey by the Council of State Social Studies Specialists revealing that 23 states mandated that all students take courses in world or global studies. New York state has redesigned several social studies courses and has required an international component to be included in the regent's exam. Arkansas has required that global perspectives be infused into the curriculum. Florida has established an office of international education. California has required human rights education in high schools and provides for international resource centers throughout the state (Baker, 1990, p. 6).

State political leaders have also taken note of the growing significance of global education. The Southern Governors Association (1986) supports the incorporation of global perspectives into the curriculum to assist students in understanding the increasing interdependence of the world's economies, nations, and cultures. Taken collectively, positions supported by communities and state organizations augur well for the future of global education. What remains to be seen is whether this impetus will be strongly felt in all classrooms in the United States.

National and International Influences on Global Education

The United States emerged from World War II with the strongest economy in the world. In 1950, the United States accounted for 59% of the world's industrial output (Wolff, Rutten, Bayers, & the World Rank Research Team, 1992, p. 24). As Japan and Germany were emerging from the ruins of the war, the economy of the United States accounted for approximately one half of the total economic output of the world.

These circumstances, while providing prosperity at home, did not particularly advance the notion of global interdependence for U.S. citizens. When one nation holds such a large share of the world's economic power, it is hard for the nation to resist the tendency to dictate instead of negotiate. Today, the United States still holds the distinction of being the nation with the world's largest economy. However, its share of the world economy today is approximately 25%. In terms of the affluence of its citizenry, the United States ranks fifth in the world behind Canada, Switzerland, Japan, and Germany (Wolff et al., 1992, p. 37).

While the United States remains among the most fortunate nations on the globe economically, its future economic position is by no means assured. If the global trends in its economy continue, the United States will need many more persons who are competent in the international economic arena. Workers will need to be literate in languages other than English and conversant with other cultures, global issues, and economic trends. A fair question to ask is, "Are there many people with these qualifications in the United States today?" If the answer is no, where will they come from in the future? There are only two possibilities: The United States can import them (there will always be some need for this), or the system of education in this country must produce them in sufficient numbers. With the economy demanding workers with a stonger background in global education, schools will have to create better global curricula than in the past.

When students in Houston, Texas, graduate from high school or college, they must be prepared to function economically, culturally, and politically—not only in Texas, but also in the rest of the nation. More so than ever before, these students must be able to function internationally, because their jobs may take them to Munich, Hong Kong, or Buenos Aires. They may work in the United States but have to work with persons or corporations from abroad. Teachers can be assured that at least some of their students will have to be functional in multicultural and global contexts; however, they will not know which ones. The only solution is to provide every student with a sufficiently broad global education so that it will not matter which students are called on to use these skills.

International forces also drive the need to provide education that is more global to U.S. students. Until the early 1990s, Canada, Mexico, and the United States charged tariffs on each other's products. Today, the three nations are bound together in the North American Free Trade Association (NAFTA), which allows goods to be produced in one nation and sold in another without facing tariffs. It is likely that the future may bring other nations in the Western

Hemisphere into a free trade association of the Americas. How does this trend influence the need for U.S. students to graduate technically competent in a field; fluent in Spanish, Portuguese, or French; and knowledgeable about other societies in North and South America? How will future international economic agreements affect the need for globally literate persons?

In 1975, under the Helsinki Accords the United States pledged to encourage the study of other cultures and foreign languages as an important means of improving global cooperation (Baker, 1990, p. 5). Living up to these accords by requiring foreign language and global education courses may not carry a great deal of weight with policy makers in U.S. education. Yet, the accords illustrate the importance other nations place on global literacy.

A final international influence, which supports pervasive global education, is the enhancement of the ability of U.S. citizens to fully understand foreign policy issues. Too often, some people in the United States discover a place on the world's map such as Kuwait, Haiti, Grenada, Bosnia, Panama, Lebanon, or Somalia only when a friend or relative is sent there on a military operation. A citizenry that places itself at risk in many corners of the world should have the educational background to fully understand the international interests of the United States in any potential conflict. A national task force on education and world views found that only 10–15% of U.S. college students could be presumed to be globally literate (Council on Learning, 1981).

If this figure is true for college students, what might the figure be when persons are included who did not attend college? This finding suggests that an extremely low percentage of U.S. citizens have the necessary international background to understand the foreign policy that directly affects them and their children. This provides one more argument for universal global education.

REDUCING PROVINCIALISM AND DEVELOPING COSMOPOLITAN PERSPECTIVES

When the major national news networks present stories occurring outside North America or Europe, they often provide viewers with a map of the region or continent with the nation in which the event is taking place highlighted. Network executives correctly assume that a major portion of the viewing public does not know where in the world the story is set without the map insert. This lack of basic geographical and global orientation is not limited to persons with general academic deficiencies. It may also be found among persons who are generally accomplished academically. Even when U.S. citizens have a general understanding of the location and significance of a nation (e.g., Nigeria), they often view that nation's population and culture as monolithic. Relatively few people in the U.S. understand that the Nigerian population is composed of persons who do not have English as a first language (like the Yoruba, Ibo, and Hausa) as well as those who speak both their native language and English. The example of Nigeria illustrates that we often view nations as being homogeneous when, in reality, they are quite heterogeneous.

The reduction of provincial attitudes is another worthy goal that may be addressed by global education. During the Reagan administration, heads of state met in Cancún, Mexico, for a dialogue on issues of development; a cartoon appeared in a Florida paper showing a poor Latin American peasant looking up at President Reagan standing on a balcony. The cartoon's caption read, "Mister, what are bootstraps?" This cartoon indicates that often persons from the developed world do not fully understand the issues facing citizens of underdeveloped nations, who are trying to survive on a few hundred dollars per year of income. In addition, solutions for economic development that have been successful in developed nations do not always translate to underdeveloped nations.

To reduce provincial attitudes and teach truly international perspectives, global education must go far beyond presenting contrasts between developed societies and underdeveloped ones. Students in the United States must also learn to understand the perspectives of developing nations. For example, if the Honduran lempira loses 20% in value against the U.S. dollar, most students would surmise that U.S. products sold in Honduras are now more expensive. They may not realize, however, that the sale of petroleum throughout the world is conducted in dollars. Consequently, the 20% devaluation of the lempira results in a significant increase in petroleum prices for Hondurans while prices for imported petroleum and its derivatives remain relatively constant in the United States. This example is well known by citizens of developing countries, but not too familiar to most U.S. citizens.

A course on regional geography of Central America might cover the topography, exports, and population of Honduras without giving U.S. students any real sense of what life is like for an average citizen of that nation. A truly global education curriculum needs to provide both a "view from the top" as well as a "view from the bottom." Without the latter, provincial and ethnocentric attitudes held by some students are more likely to persist.

Another example of limited information leading to skewed opinions can be found when trying to answer the question, "Why are developing countries poor?" To paraphrase the cartoon cited earlier, "Why don't they lift themselves up by the bootstraps?" One striking characteristic of nearly all developing countries is that they have a very high percentage (50–90%) of the population employed in agriculture. (This contrasts with slightly under 3% for the United States.)

Why don't developing nations adopt the U.S. agricultural techniques that have made the U.S. agricultural sector the leader of the world? The success of U.S. agriculture rests largely on four foundations: irrigation, a high degree of mechanization, ample use of fertilizers, and the ability to use pesticides to minimize crop loss to insects. In addition, much of the agriculture in the United States enjoys the advantage of having large tracts of flat land where the use of farm machinery, fertilizers and pesticides are more efficient. How many of these factors are accessible to a small farmer in Latin America, Africa, or Asia? How much capital is required to achieve the efficiency enjoyed by U.S. agriculture even if large tracts of land could be obtained by small farmers in the developing world?

Often, naive or provincial attitudes are developed by students who judge issues in other nations by the standards of what is familiar. Global education which discusses the heterogeneous nature of other nations and the "view from the bottom" in developing nations can be a strong antidote against provincialism.

Schools are not the only purveyors of global information. Television has become the major source of news, domestic and international, for citizens of the United States. Bearing this in mind, the comparison of television news in different nations in Figure 1.2 is particularly insightful. While the comparisons do not distinguish between domestic and international content in news, the very large gap between the United States and other Western nations in television

FIGURE 1.2   News as a Percentage
of All Television
Programming

New Zealand	73%
Denmark	43%
Canada	32%
Netherlands	25%
Australia	21%
Germany	20%
Italy	18%
United Kingdom	17%
France	17%
Japan	6%
United States	2%

Reprinted from Wolff, M., Rutten, P., Bayers, A., &
the World Bank Research Team. (1992). *Where we
stand: Can America make it in the global race for the
wealth, health, and happiness?* New York: Bantam
Books, pp. 68–69.

news presentation is a cause for some concern. Even if one considers
that U.S. television networks are commercial in nature, while governments may subsidize other nations' television networks, the gap in
the availability of television news remains high. Provincial attitudes
inhibit international economic competitiveness, impede understanding of foreign policy issues, and prevent Americans from acquiring a
thorough understanding of the complexity of the world. Perhaps the
desire for simplicity, albeit an artificial simplicity, is responsible for
the development and maintenance of provincial attitudes.

The vignettes that follow are illustrative of the idea that provincialism can affect both the famous and the not so famous. They are
not intended to degrade the national image. Their purpose is to suggest to the reader that the United States can do better at acquiring
global literacy in all levels of society.

Ronald Takaki, an eminent U.S. historian, arrived in Norfolk,
Virginia, to attend a conference. During the ride to the hotel the taxi
driver asked, "How long have you been in this country?" Takaki responded, "All my life, I was born in the United States." He further

explained that his immigrant grandfather came from Japan, and the family had been in the United States for over 100 years. The taxi driver replied, "I was wondering, because your English is excellent!" (Takaki, 1993, p. 1).

Takaki's taxi driver demonstrated a homogeneous view of a heterogeneous nation, in this case, the United States. It is highly unlikely that Takaki's taxi driver was aware of cultural diversity in the populations of other nations if he was unaware of the Asian American dimension of his own country.

Sensitivity to language and cultural differences is very important. This is especially true in the political arena. During the late 1970s, U.S. President Carter was visiting a number of European countries. One stop on the tour was Warsaw, Poland. During the speech, Carter remarked in English that "The American people have a great love for the Polish people." After the Polish translation, a titter ran through the crowd. Apparently, the less-than-perfect translation was, "The American people have a great lust for the Polish people."

When former Senator Paul Simon was a member of the U.S. House of Representatives, he visited the United States embassy in Cairo, Egypt. From there, he boarded a car with some embassy staff members for a meeting with Egyptian President Anwar Sadat. Simon's party arrived quite late for the meeting, because none of the embassy staff members spoke enough Arabic to convey their destination to the Egyptian driver.

Over two decades ago, Chevrolet wanted to introduce a new automobile model, the Nova, to nations in the Caribbean and Latin America. Sales of the new automobile were very sluggish. Corporate officials then learned that "No va" meant, "It doesn't go." People were not flocking to purchase a car with a name suggesting mechanical unreliability. The car was then reintroduced as the Chevrolet Carib and proceeded to sell normally.

During the latter part of the Bush administration, President Bush decided to visit a number of Pacific Rim nations. One of the first stops was Australia, a nation that shares a common language and some cultural similarities with the United States. As Bush's motorcade proceeded along a broad avenue of Canberra, the Australian capital, the sides of the road were lined with well wishers waving at the U.S. president. President Bush waved back and then decided to change to a Winston Churchill-like V sign with his fingers. The Australian public was quite perplexed, because a V sign is regarded as an obscene gesture in their nation.

During the Reagan administration, the U.S. ambassador to Indonesia decided to invite the Indonesian foreign minister for dinner at the embassy in Jakarta. The invitation occurred during the Muslim holy month of Ramadan. When dinner was served, the Indonesian foreign minister, a Muslim, would not eat. The main course consisted of pork, a meat forbidden for consumption by the *Koran*, which is the holy book of Islam.

These anecdotes, taken collectively, show that a lack of cultural and global literacy can have significant economic and political repercussions. Provincial attitudes can result in consequences from an embarrassing diplomatic incident to a foreign student feeling less than welcome in a U.S. school. By citing these incidents demonstrating a lack of cultural or global sophistication, the authors do not intend to suggest that such events are unique to people from the U.S. Even if one accepts the "other nations are probably doing similar things" rationale, it is patently clear that provincialism does not advance the political, cultural, or economic interests of the United States or its image as a great nation. Global education for all U.S. citizens cannot guarantee an end to provincial attitudes and cultural indifference, but it can be a strong agent to minimize them.

In examining the influences on global education, a correlation emerges: "The more students know about global affairs, the more positive their attitudes" (Tye & Tye, 1983, p. 53). Not only is the acquisition of knowledge about global issues affected by students' attitudes but also society's attitudes toward providing a strong global education curriculum.

This chapter has provided a number of examples at the leadership level suggesting that global education should be much more incorporated into the core curriculum than it is. Why has this not occurred? Perhaps support for global literacy at the leadership level is not shared with equal enthusiasm at the grass roots level. General support for global education may begin to wane once all concerned become aware of the "heavy lifting" required to make global education ubiquitous in U.S. classrooms. Another possibility may be that people will decide it is easier to "let them learn about us."

Without a doubt, the need—or lack of a need—to be globally literate is related to a nation's power and position. It could be argued that it is far more important for the people of Finland to learn English than for the population of the U.S. to master Finnish; for example, trading with the United States is more important to Finland than vice versa. The importance for U.S. citizens to be multiculturally and globally literate may have been less than for citizens of other nations, but it is becoming far less true and will be more problematic in the twenty-first century.

Also, citizens of the United States benefit from the fact that English was a colonial language. Because of Great Britain's empire that once established itself and English on several continents, contemporary speakers of English have an advantage over speakers of other languages. Languages which are predominant tend to have a large number of speakers and represent nations with significant economic power. It was, after all, colonization that made some languages international and others not.

The national preoccupation with standardized testing has not augured well for global education in the United States. The key sections of the SAT, ACT, and general GRE, tests required for most university study, give students no additional points for global literacy; what is being measured is largely verbal and quantitative ability. What would happen to the global education curriculum in elementary and secondary schools if colleges and universities with limited enrollments began to require a standardized test of global literacy for admission?

Another force which has not aided global education is the "back-to-basics" movement, which emphasizes basic math and verbal skills. There is nothing inherently contradictory between global literacy and a mastery of basic verbal and quantitative skills. However, the back-to-basics movement in the United States has not defined global education as basic or foundational knowledge. Although many other nations have defined second language and global literacy as important basic knowledge, these areas are often considered to be electives in the American curriculum.

Simon (1980) lamented the woeful state of foreign language education in the United States; he began his book with this facetious suggestion: "We should erect a sign at each port of entry into the United States, 'Welcome to the United States. We cannot speak your language.'" (Simon, 1980, p. 1). As the twenty-first century dawns, there has not been appreciable change in U.S. curriculum to offset

Simon's comment. Before more significant progress is made promoting second language and global literacy in the United States, educators and the public must be convinced that progress in these two areas does not mean a loss of English fluency or national pride (Thomas & Collier, 1996). To the extent that this false dichotomy exists in the minds of U.S. citizens, progress in global education will suffer. The challenge of providing a truly global education must be met so that U.S. students can develop civic responsibility within their nation as well as feel a strong kinship with the rest of humanity.

SUMMARY

While the fields of global and multicultural education have some overlap in content, global education concentrates on material about nations other than the student's, while multicultural education focuses on understanding cultural diversity within the nation. Global and multicultural education both share the curricular goal of presenting content from multiple perspectives. This approach yields a richer understanding for students.

Teacher attitudes are a very significant factor in the success or failure of global and multicultural education. Preliminary surveys of teacher attitudes toward these two fields provide mixed results, but there is a consensus that most teachers need additional training to master the content in global education. There are also some concerns that a global focus in the curriculum must come at the expense of national pride.

The selection of academic content in global education is very important. Students need to understand traditional geographic, economic, and political concepts and facts (mainstream knowledge) in order to analyze international issues. It is equally important for students to be exposed to perspectives that sometimes challenge mainstream knowledge and that students be asked to examine issues from the perspectives of other nations besides their own (transformational knowledge). When educators present transformational knowledge in their classrooms, students will invariably be exposed to some controversial issues. Research indicates that students who are exposed to controversial issues in an open and positive classroom atmosphere develop a greater sense of political efficacy and positive global attitudes. Therefore, the attitudinal realm in global education plays a significant role in the cognitive domain.

In recent years, many states have taken affirmative steps to promote global education. Political leaders are realizing that the United States needs more globally literate citizens to succeed in the international economy. Academic organizations have also supported global education in their professional standards and publications. The provision of global education is now among the standards that must be met for the accreditation of many of this nation's colleges of education.

While isolationist or provincial perspectives may have been prevalent in the past, they do not serve the United States well for the future. Provincial attitudes can have negative consequences on economic, political, cultural, and educational matters. Providing a global education curriculum that results in globally literate citizens depends largely on how educators feel about accepting this challenge.

QUESTIONS FOR REFLECTION

1. Given the definitions of global and multicultural education provided in this chapter, why do you think that there is some confusion about the scope of each field? What are some areas of overlap?

2. How would you describe teacher attitudes toward multicultural and global education? How significant are teacher attitudes to successful teaching in each field?

3. What portions of your own education have consisted of mainstream and transformative knowledge? What reasons can you give for this ratio?

4. Identify two examples of transformative knowledge in global education and two more in multicultural education. Give a reason for selecting each example.

5. What happens to students' views of the world when teachers avoid controversial issues?

6. What are some positive consequences of teaching controversial issues in an open, analytical, and comfortable classroom?

7. What are some barriers to implementing global and/or multicultural education? What suggestions can you give to overcome each of the barriers you identified?

8. "Teaching about global issues minimizes students' concerns about their own country." Support or refute this statement and give at least two reasons for your position.

9. A number of governmental organizations and academic societies have taken steps to support global education. Give three reasons why you think these groups have advocated global education.

10. Explain in your own terms what is meant by teaching the "view from the top" and "view from the bottom" when teaching a global curriculum.

11. Explain two consequences of the lack of global literacy in the international, political, cultural, or economic arenas. How significant is global literacy in advancing the interests of any nation?

12. Assume you have been selected superintendent of a school district that lacks a significant global education component in its curriculum. What steps would you take in order to incorporate global education into the curriculum? What obstacles might you face in this effort?

13. How does a nation's size, geographic position, and economic power relate to the probability that its educational system will produce globally literate citizens?

14. Traditionally, global literacy has not been defined as a basic skill in the schools of the United States. How would you attempt to persuade a back-to-basics advocate that global education is needed today in U.S. education?

REFERENCES

Alexandre, L. (1989, Winter). Genderizing international studies: Revisioning concepts and curriculum. *International Studies Notes, 14*(1) 5–8.

American Association for the Advancement of Science. (1989, March 1). Curriculum proposals from "Science for all Americans." *Education Week, 8*(23), 122–123.

Baker, F. J. (1990, March). *Internationalizing public education: Past practices, present programs, and future promises.* Paper presented at the annual conference of the Comparative and International Education Society. (ERIC Document Reproduction Service No. ED 327 432)

Banks, J. A. (1994). *Multiethnic education: Theory and practice* (3rd ed.). Boston: Allyn & Bacon.

Bennett, C. (1995). *Comprehensive multicultural education.* Boston: Allyn & Bacon.

Cole, D. J. (1984). Multicultural and global education: A possible merger. *Theory into Practice, 23*(2), 151–154.

Council on Learning. (1981). *Task force statement on education and world view.* New Rochelle, NY. (ERIC Document Reproduction Service No. 203 826).

Diaz, C. F. (1992). Resistance to multicultural education: Concerns and responses. In C.F. Diaz. (Ed.), *Multicultural Education for the Twenty-First Century* (pp. 193–202). Washington, DC: National Education Association.

Dorman, W. A. (1992, August). *The not so odd couple: Critical thinking and global education.* Paper presented at the Annual International Conference for Critical Thinking and Moral Critique, Rohnert Park, CA. (ERIC Document Reproduction Service No. ED 371 980)

Evans, C. (1987). Teaching a global perspective in elementary classrooms. *The Elementary School Journal, 87*(5), 545–555.

Fain, S. M. (1988, Fall). Revising the American character: Perspectives on global education and multicultural education. *Louisiana Social Studies Journal, 15*(1), 26–33.

Ford, M. (1979). *The Development of an Instrument for Assessing Levels of Ethnicity in Public School Teachers.* Unpublished doctoral dissertation, University of Houston, TX.

Gollnick, D. M. (1992). Multicultural education: Policies and practices in teacher education. In C. Grant. (Ed.), *Research and multicultural education: From the margins to the mainstream* (pp. 218–239). Washington, DC: Falmer.

Gollnick, D. M., & Chinn, P. C. (1998). *Multicultural Education in a Pluralistic Society* (5th ed.). Upper Saddle River, NJ: Merrill/Prentice-Hall.

Goodlad, J. (1984). *A place called school: Prospects for the future.* New York: McGraw-Hill.

Grosvenor, G. M. (1989, December). Superpowers are not so super in geography. *National Geographic, 183,* 816–818.

Herman, W. (1983). Scope and sequence in social studies education: What should be taught when? *Social Education, 47,* 94–100.

Kobus, D. K. (1992). Multicultural/global education: An educational agenda for the rights of the child. *Social Education, 56*(4), 224–227.

Merryfield, M. M. (1991). Preparing American secondary social studies teachers to teach with a global perspective: A status report. *Journal of Teacher Education, 42*(1), 11–20.

National Commission on Social Studies in the Schools. (1989). *Charting a course: Social studies curriculum for the twenty-first century.* Washington, DC: Author.

National Council for the Social Studies (NCSS). (1982). Position statement on global education. *Social Education, 46*(1), 36–38.

O'Brien, A., & Sreberny-Mohammadi, A. (1993, April/May). Engendering world studies. *Social Studies, 84*(2), 74–77.

Simon, P. (1980). *The tongue-tied American: Confronting the foreign language crisis.* New York: Continuum.

Soley, M. (1996). If it's controversial, why teach it? *Social Education, 60*(1), 9–10.

Southern Governor's Association Advisory Council. (1986). *International education, cornerstone of competition.* Washington, DC: Author.

Takaki, R. (1993). *A different mirror: A history of multicultural America.* Boston: Little, Brown & Company.

Thomas, W. P., & Collier, V. (1996, May 1). Language-minority student achievement and program effectiveness. *National Association for Bilingual Education News,* 33–35.

Tiedt, P. L., & Tiedt, I. L. (1995). *Multicultural teaching: A handbook of activities, information, and resources* (4th ed.). Boston: Allyn & Bacon.

Tucker, J. (1983). Teacher attitudes toward global education: A report from Dade county. *Educational Research Quarterly, 8*(1), 65–77.

Tye, B., & Tye, K. (1983). Global education research: A partial agenda for the future. *Educational Research Quarterly, 8*(1), 48–54.

Wolff, M., Rutten, P., Bayers, A., & the World Bank Research Team. (1992). *Where we stand: Can America make it in the global race for the wealth, health, and happiness?* New York: Bantam Books.

2

AN INQUIRY FRAMEWORK
FOR STUDYING GLOBAL ISSUES

Major Points

- The meaning of "globalization" is explained.
- Suggestions are offered on how global studies can be part of daily curriculum lessons.
- The chapter proposes the systematic construction of categories of educational objectives focusing on global studies and makes a case for the division of objectives for global education into cognitive, affective, and participatory domains.
- An example of a table of specifications that seeks to delimit the field of global education is presented for classroom use.
- The connection of educational objectives and classroom strategies is provided clearly.
- Examples of inquiry strategies in dealing with global concepts and issues in the classroom are offered.

Globalization, as stated by Featherstone et al., refers "both to the compression of the world and to the intensification of the consciousness of the world as a whole" (p. 70). This process is ongoing and all of us, young and old, Westerners and nonWesterners, are inescapably involved in it. The compression of the world is real. People witness it in their daily lives, in the foods they eat, in the TV programs they watch, in the cars they drive, in their dresses and costumes, in the people they choose to govern them, and so on.

Globalization as a sociopolitical phenomenon is here to stay. Educators have the responsibility to provide user-friendly school environments so that children develop the appropriate cognitive skills to understand and explain the globalization process and to critically analyze its impact on their lives and the lives of people around them. Understanding what is involved in globalization, however, including globalization's short and long range effects on humans, is not enough. There needs to be a consciousness of the world as a whole, a consciousness that the human species is inextricably bonded together and that each person is, in fact, a member of the world community. By developing and promoting the feeling and the attitude that above all people are citizens of the world, people will have compassion for and understand their world brethren and fellow citizens. The global consciousness emerges when they begin to value the world culture and develop cosmopolitan rather than provincial orientations.

The process through which the concept and value of globalization is delivered to students is known as global education. The overall goal of global education is to provide, through instruction, opportunities for students to understand globalization as a complicated and richly developed concept. The development of a global consciousness carries the proviso that such consciousness is individualistic and idiosyncratic. No special model is to be imposed on students by a teacher or another agent. With an understanding of the global environment and the internationalization of a global consciousness, students also need to develop strong social participation skills so that they are involved in making the decisions affecting them. In other words, students need to know how to impact the global system as world citizens and as advocates of a well-grounded position or point of view.

INSTRUCTIONAL OBJECTIVES
FOR GLOBAL EDUCATION

In the material that follows, examples of suggested instructional objectives for global education are presented. Using these as a basis, teachers may develop their own objectives in the global education classroom.

The authors of this book are committed to providing an instructional model for global education based on the philosophy of inquiry. Inquiry teaching seeks to empower the individual to engage in the judicious exploration of alternatives, be these alternatives in the form of hypotheses explaining the world or in the form of value judgments that the individual is in a position to defend. Inquiry teaching, however, goes beyond the cognitive and the affective domains. It seeks to involve students in social and political participation. Through such participation, citizens can individually or collectively seek to change aspects of the world around them. As they take action, they develop the attitude that in some measure they control their socio-political environment—rather than being controlled by it.

Several years ago Benjamin Bloom and his associates developed certain taxonomies in order to categorize and clarify educational objectives. The original taxonomies placed all educational objectives obtained through a national survey under three categories: cognitive, affective, and psychomotor. The cognitive category of the taxonomies emphasized educational objectives that related to the acquisition of knowledge and to the understanding of concepts (Bloom, Englehart, Furst, Hill, & Krathwohl, 1956). The affective domain of the taxonomies included educational objectives that centered on feelings, attitudes, and values (Krathwohl, Bloom, & Masia, 1964). The psychomotor domain classified educational objectives that dealt with the physical or manipulative aspects of learning and instruction, such as learning to play a sport or acting out in a theatrical performance (Harrow, 1972). A fourth domain, called the participatory domain, was developed to include educational objectives that dealt with skills students needed to affect decisions such as *proposing* a new course of action and *mobilizing* support for it (Massialas & Hurst, 1978).

Although the taxonomies were prepared many years ago, they continue to be used by teachers and other education personnel in the quest to plan and formulate clear educational objectives. Referring to Bloom's taxonomy, two educators involved in presenting effective instructional models state, "Though more than 40 years old, the taxonomy has been used in a variety of settings to analyze objectives, classroom questions, text problems, exercises, and test items" (Kauchak & Eggen, 1998, p. 166). Bloom's taxonomy was the first of its kind to be used by others. It is the "most widely used tax-onomy" in the field and "by far the most popular" (Worthen, Borg, & White, 1993, pp. 244–245).

To accompany the taxonomies, Bloom and his associates pro-moted the use of "tables of specifications," which are a means of connecting skills in the various domains with subject matter. The subject matter can be biology, chemistry, mathematics, geography, history, or English. The key concepts in these subjects naturally are different. In the area of skills, however, the differences are minimal.

An example of a table of specifications based on Bloom's ideas of classifying educational objectives is presented in Figure 2.1 on pages 42–43. Note that the authors of this book do not subscribe to the belief that teachers should mechanistically use tables of specifi-cations or classify educational objectives under the four domains. Figure 2.1 is primarily for the purposes of illustration and clarifica-tion, in order to assist with the development of objectives that are meaningful and can be implemented in the classroom. Such organi-zation allows for a systematic program of measurement and evalua-tion. Teachers are normally asked in their weekly lesson plans to state the objectives specific to their subjects. Figure 2.1 may help them construct their objectives, objectives that for the purposes of this book will relate to global issues and concerns. It should be un-derstood, however, that the choice of lesson objectives is strictly a teacher choice, since teachers best know their subject matter and the special needs of their students.

Another reason for developing the table of specifications is to offer an example of an attempt to delimit the field of global studies or global education. The authors hope that others will follow this effort so that the important concepts and methods of inquiry in glo-bal education can be identified, clarified, and made accessible to the classroom teacher. Teachers may use the sample table of specifica-tions presented here wholly or partially, or they may construct their own.

Figure 2.1 presents an example of how the objectives for global education can be structured. Instructional objectives are generated through the intersection of the substantive (vertical column) and procedural (horizontal column) dimensions. The substantive di-mension is comprised of concepts and generalizations formed through interdisciplinary work in the field of global studies. In these examples, substantive concepts are divided into two main categories. Category 1.0 focuses on the idea of a world system and how this system behaves and has behaved over the years. Category 2.0 deals with the world subsystems, these being divided into four categories: political, economic, social, and ecological. These subsystems can be subdivided further. For example, the world political system can include the categories of power, legitimacy, selection of world leaders, citizen participation, and rule enforcement. (This is by no means a definitive list of substantive concepts or topics for world studies.) Teachers can develop their own lists, focusing on those concepts considered most relevant to the students. It should be pointed out, however, that while the social science disciplines may provide much of the substance of instruction, the experiences that students—as individuals or in groups—bring to the classroom are as valuable and provide another important source of content. Student experiences in world affairs constitute a bona fide source of content in formulating and implementing classroom objectives.

The behavioral, or skill, dimension in the matrix (Figure 2.1) consists of processes and actions students engage in as they pursue the study of the substantive concepts of world systems. The behaviors or processes students may engage in include the cognitive, the participatory, and the affective domains. The cognitive domain emphasizes the skills that individuals need to have in order to explain how the world system operates. Key skills in this domain are the forming and testing of hypotheses. In the process of testing hypotheses, students learn how to detect, screen, and analyze data. These data can be quantitative or qualitative.

The affective domain deals with attitudes and values. The evaluative category is, in a way, an extension of the cognitive domain, because value positions are supported based on explicit reasons. The normative category deals with the application of ethical standards or norms to decisions about world problems. Value judgments are made here about world events, and these judgments are prompted by the moral criteria of each individual. The attitudinal category encompasses the range of predispositions students develop toward their environment. Some of these predispositions or attitudes develop as a result of instruction focusing on world systems.

Participatory skills are skills that individuals need to have in order to participate in decisions affecting them. Since the process of globalization is a worldwide phenomenon affecting every person, participatory skills are extremely important, both for the individual

FIGURE 2.1 Table of Specifications, Global Systems

Substantive Experiential			Skills
Cognitive		A	Making Distinctions
		B	Demonstrating Conceptual Understanding
		C	Identifying a Problem
		D	Stating a Problem
		E	Forming a Hypothesis
		F	Exploring Consequences
		G	Collecting Relevant Data
		H	Analyzing Data
		I	Testing Ideas
		J	Making a Generalization
		K	Applying a Generalization
Participatory		L	Observing
		M	Supporting
		N	Proposing
		O	Mobilizing
		P	Organizing
		Q	Cost–benefit Analysis
		R	Bargaining/Negotiating
		S	Rule Making
		T	Voting
Affective	Evaluative	U	Identifying an Issue
		V	Taking a Defensible Position
		W	Grounding a Position
	Normative	X	Empathizing
		Y	Being Fair
		Z	Promoting Equality
		AA	Applying Justice
	Attitudinal	BB	Being Objective
		CC	Showing Interest
		DD	Showing Trust
		EE	Being Efficacious
		FF	Showing a Sense of Social Integration
		GG	Demonstrating Cross-cultural Awareness

	1.0 Concepts of a World System	2.0 World Subsystems	2.1 Political World Subsystem	2.2 Economic World Subsystem	2.3 Social World Subsystem	2.4 Ecological World Subsystem

and for the group in which the individual holds membership. According to the category system in Figure 2.1, skills in this domain begin with the simple act of observing world phenomena, such as the crises in the former Yugoslavia, in Chechneya, and in Cyprus, followed by taking an active role in proposing solutions. Students can learn that they have the power and the right on many of these issues to go beyond their classroom and their school. They can reach world decision-making bodies such as the United Nations Security Council, the Council of Europe, the International Court of Justice, the World Bank, United Nations Educational, Scientific, and Cultural Organization (UNESCO), and those who dispense information through the Internet and other world media. As world consciousness is formed, students feel competent and seek out opportunities to participate directly in world affairs.

The overall purpose of the table of specifications in this chapter is to develop instructional objectives that, if implemented properly in the classroom, can enable students to attain proficiency in their interactions with their world sociopolitical environment.

As mentioned earlier, each square in the matrix can generate an instructional objective. For example, the intersection of "1.0 Concepts of a World System" with "E, Forming a Hypothesis" can generate a behavioral objective such as, "Given instruction on the subject, students should be able to develop a hypothesis which explains how the world as a whole operates as one entity, as a system." Another example, in the affective domain and using the concepts of a world system intersecting with the norm of "Z, Promoting Equality," could be, "Given appropriate instruction on the subject, students should be able to apply principles of equality to certain acts by the world governmental bodies."

It is primarily the instructor's responsibility to provide the setting and the materials in the classroom in order to attain such objectives. Materials need not be just the textbooks, although even a traditional text can be used as an initial springboard for group or individual thinking and for acting. Newspaper articles, videos, pictures, computer programs, lectures, student and faculty experiences, comic strips, musical selections, and laboratory experiments can all be used as springboards involving students in the process of inquiry into world matters and concerns. The important thing to remember when selecting classroom materials is to make sure that these materials relate to the relevant instructional objectives. When classroom procedures are related to objectives and followed by an appropriate assessment program, instruction on world affairs evolves in a systematic and effective manner.

IMPLEMENTING THE OBJECTIVES

In this section, a series of examples are presented suggesting ways in which the classroom teacher can use various springboards to implement the objectives of the world systems in action. Using these examples as models, teachers can select their own materials to match the age level of their students and the school environment in which they operate.

Example 1: Inquiring into the Environment and Population Growth

This classroom activity focuses primarily on the ecological world system dimensions (Category 2.4 in Figure 2.1). The whole range of cognitive, affective, and participatory skills and processes can be employed in the execution of this unit. Classroom inquiry may commence through the introduction of two sets of data as presented in Figure 2.2 and Figure 2.3 (on page 47).

For this activity, the instructor is initially interested in creating opportunities for students to hypothesize about the impact of population growth on different areas of the environment, such as landscape, food production and consumption, pollution levels, and water resources. Figure 2.2, "Different Futures," provides various scenarios. This activity is based on "The Environment and Population Growth: Decade for Action," in *Population Reports* (1992), and projects population growth until the year 2100. The material is to be used as a springboard to create interest among the students and prompt them to think about this issue, an issue that has global ramifications. For example, inquiry-generating questions to be asked by the instructor of the students in examining Figure 2.2 include the following:

1. What does the chart tell us about population growth?
2. Are the growth patterns between developed and developing regions the same or different? Why or why not?

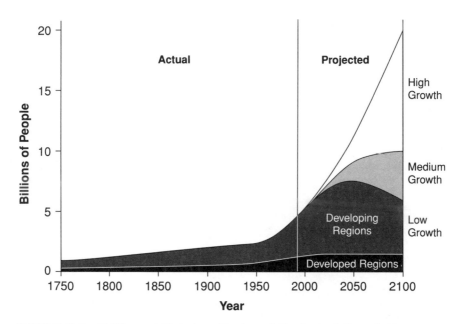

FIGURE 2.2   Different Futures: Past and Projected Population Growth, 1750–2100

UN projections show that differing paths of population growth beginning in 1990 could lead to a world population as high as 19 billion in the year 2100 or as low as 6 billion. The low growth projection assumes that fertility eventually stabilizes at 1.7 children per woman. The medium projection assumes fertility eventually stabilizes at 2.1. The high projection assumes fertility eventually stabilizes at 2.5.

From Green, C. P. (1992, May). The environment and population growth: Decade for action. *Population Reports, M*(10), 5. Reprinted by permission of the Johns Hopkins University Press.

3. What would happen in the world if the high growth population projection for the year 2100 materializes?
4. What would happen if low growth or medium growth were attained?
5. What would be the effects on various aspects of the environment if the different growth patterns prevailed, for example, on food production and consumption, potable water resources, smog production, urban sprawl, and health?
6. What do your own experiences indicate about the impact of population changes on your community?

		Low-Income Countries with Limited Ability to Import Food		Countries Able to Afford Food Imports*	

Countries Able to Feed Less than Half of Year 2000 Population		**Africa**
		Burundi
		Cape Verdi
		Comoros
		Ethiopia
		Lesotho
		Mauritania
		Namibia
		Réunion
		Rwanda
		Somalia
		Uganda
		Western Sahara
		
		Asia
		(None)
			Latin America and Caribbean
			Antigua
			Barbados
			Guadeloupe
			Haiti
			Martinique
			Netherlands
			  Antilles
			Winward Islands
			
			Near East and North Africa
			Yemen
				Africa
				Kenya
				Mauritius
				Niger
				Nigeria
				
				Asia
				Afghanistan
				Singapore
					Latin America and Caribbean
					El Salvador
					
					Near East and North Africa
					Algeria
					Bahrain
					Iraq
					Israel
					Jordan
					Kuwait
					Lebanon
					Oman
					Qatar
					Saudi Arabia
					United
					  Arab Emirates

Countries Able to Feed 50% to 99% of Year 2000 Population		**Africa**
		Benin
		Botswana
		Burkina Faso
		Malawi
		Sierra Leone
		Swaziland
		Togo
		
		Asia
		Bhutan
		Vietnam
			Latin America and Caribbean
			Bahamas
			
			Near East and North Africa
			(None)
				Africa
				Senegal
				Zimbabwe
				
				Asia
				Bangladesh
				Philippines
				Sri Lanka
					Latin America and Caribbean
					Dominican
					  Republic
					Guatemala
					Jamaica
					Trinidad
					  and Tobago
					
					Near East and North Africa
					Iran
					Morocco
					Syria
					Tunisia

FIGURE 2.3   Not Enough Food: Countries Unable to Feed Their Projected Populations without Food Imports in the Year 2000

*Countries with manufactured exports of over US $100 million in 1979 or 1980 or with significant wealth in fuel minerals.

Source: United Nations Food and Agriculture Organization

From Green, C. P. (1992, May). The environment and population growth: Decade for action. *Population Reports, M*(10), 9. The United Nations is the author of the original material. Reprinted by permission of the United Nations.

These questions are likely to trigger student thinking about a major world phenomenon: population growth. This phenomenon has immediate implications for individuals and the communities in which they live. As the various hypotheses are developed, the teacher must keep asking for grounds to support these hypotheses. Both logical and empirical grounds are sought. To answer these questions, students inescapably get immersed in relevant data collection and analysis. They seek to test their hypotheses by collecting the best possible data and by drawing on their own personal experiences. The students should eventually realize that the reasons why some countries cannot provide enough food for their people are complex. There are internal factors, for example, affecting how a society distributes its resources (equity or equality factors). There are also external factors, including what the world community can do to bring about a balance between "have" and "have not" countries.

Figure 2.3, "Not Enough Food," clearly illustrates one of the consequences of projected population growth for the year 2000. Here the students may begin with cognitive questions and then raise questions in both the affective and participatory domains. Initially, the key affective questions are as follows:

1. Do you believe it is fair for the people of the countries listed in Figure 2.3 to suffer from hunger?
2. How do you personally feel toward these people?
3. How would you feel if you were in their shoes?
4. Is it just for the developed world to allow this situation to continue?
5. What is the issue in this case?
6. What is your position on the issue and how do you defend it?

Following this value-based discussion, questions likely to elicit social and political participation include the following:

1. Do your own observations or experiences in these countries confirm the report provided in Figure 2.3?
2. What proposals for action can you make, and to whom, to alleviate the problem as you perceive it?
3. On what grounds would you support your proposal?
4. How would you mobilize support for your proposal?

5. How would you organize the actions to be taken by you and your supporters to bring about change and a possible resolution to the problem?
6. How would you go about negotiating various ways for resolving the problem with the respective decision makers?
7. What would be the loss or gain in using various means to approach the relevant agencies and decision makers?
8. What actions have you taken to implement your goals?
9. How successful were you?
10. What additional actions would you take?

For this activity, the instructor should be able to provide materials that can be used as data by students to plan action strategies. For example, a draft information handout released by the UN on September 9, 1994, may be helpful. This material is entitled *Program of Action of the United Nations, International Conference on Population and Development.* If computer facilities are available, many of these materials can be accessed through the Internet.

This exercise for use with Figure 2.3 is intended to involve students in all aspects of decision making concerning a major world issue (e.g., population growth and the environment). Additional materials can be provided to enable students to immerse themselves in discussions on important world concerns. Cognitive, affective, and participatory skills are thus strengthened to meet the overall instructional goal—understanding the operations of the world system and developing a consciousness of being a member of the world citizenry.

Example 2: World Financial Markets

This inquiry-based lesson may begin by presenting to the students a picture of people working in a stock exchange (Figure 2.4). This particular picture actually represents the Cairo Stock Exchange that was formed in 1883. So that this springboard may be used as a "discovery episode," the teacher does not reveal the location of the stock exchange.

The inquiry generated by this springboard, clearly refers to "2.2 Economic World Subsystem," in the table of specifications (Figure 2.1). Beginning with cognitive objectives, Categories A–K, the teacher may begin to ask the following questions:

FIGURE 2.4

Illustration by Norman MacDonald. (1996, January/February). *Aramco World, 47*(1), 6–7.
Reprinted by permission of *Aramco World.*

1. What does this picture refer to? (discovery question)
2. What is this picture all about? (hypothesis-generating question)
3. On what grounds do you support your hypothesis? (asking for reasons, evidence)
4. What may be some comparable situations that you know of? (asking students to collect more data or to bring out their personal experiences)

These initial questions based on the visual representation of information create interest among the students and set the tone for exploring the globalization of stock exchanges. In fact, students may have a difficult time identifying the stock exchange in the picture as being located in a Middle Eastern city, since it resembles a stock exchange in any part of the world. Students may observe that modern furniture and computers are being used, and the men and women at work here have Western attire. The only details that may reveal more about the identity of the facility is Arabic writing on the large ticker screens and the relatively small size of the exchange. Given this springboard, students can begin to talk about stock exchanges and their functions in the world. The aim of this initial material is not to specify the location of the exchange but to discuss the idea that such exchanges have now become a universal phenomenon. For example, a crash in one of the exchanges (for instance, Hong Kong) has immediate ramifications in all of the world markets.

To follow up on the picture, students may be asked to read the following excerpt from Josh Martin's 1996 article "Taking Stock" and analyze it with the sample questions listed after the passage:

Taking Stock*

Throughout the region, impressive growth rates are catching the attention of the would-be investors and fueling pressure for further change. According to International Finance Corporation figures, the Arab exchanges, like many other emerging markets, are expected to outperform their long-established counterparts in the U.S., Europe and Japan in the coming years. Worldwide, growth among 20 emerging markets has generally exceeded that of the 9 largest developed markets. In Morocco and Tunisia, for example, stock market investors realized annual returns ranging between 20 and 30 percent in both 1993 and 1994, more than double the returns in better-known world markets.

Throughout the Middle East, international investment is now widely regarded as one key to national economic growth— yet historically, the Middle East has been "under-lent." In the early 1990s, the *Wall Street Journal* reports, when international capital flows to emerging markets exceeded $200 billion, only three percent was going to the Middle East, including the Gulf region. Especially in relatively volatile, high-growth markets,

---

*Excerpt from Martin, J. (1996, January/February). Taking stock. *Aramco World*, 47(1), 2–11. Reprinted by permission of *Aramco World*.

stability and investor confidence result from a careful balancing of the freedom to invest, on the one hand, and the control of speculation on the other.

In Bahrain, the BSE [Bahrain Stock Exchange] has opened to foreign investment in cautious stages. Then, in 1990, the BSE permitted outside investors to trade in shares of the Arab Banking Corporation, one of the largest financial institutions in the Gulf. Non-resident foreigners were then able to invest in four banking firms out of the total 32 issues on the BSE. Investors from more than 26 countries now hold shares in one or more of those institutions.

In July 1994, the BSE relaxed the regulations further. Now, foreigners resident in Bahrain may buy and sell in any of the 32 listed companies—but foreign holdings cannot exceed 24 percent of any company's outstanding shares, and no single individual or foreign institution can hold more than one percent of the shares of any company. Officials say even these restrictions are likely to be lifted further as the BSE completes its linkage with Oman's Muscat Securities Exchange, a move begun in 1993 and aimed at creating a combined market with 130 listed companies and a $7 billion capitalization.

One innovative way Middle Eastern markets can build a diverse international investor base is a relatively new form of mutual funds that specializes in one region of the world or in one specific country. These "country funds" are designed specifically to attract international capital. Their investments spread across a variety of long-established and newly privatized firms, domestic securities and government treasury bills in their region or country, but the funds themselves are traded on the London, New York, and Tokyo stock exchanges.

Worldwide there are now more than 150 such funds, representing more than $30 billion in capital; two decades ago, they numbered only a handful. But as yet only a few operate on the periphery of the Arab world, in India, Pakistan, and Turkey. Within the Arab world, leading stock exchanges have begun their development of mutual funds with several "closed-end" funds—a type that puts a ceiling on capitalization—which are expected to be offered in Bahrain, Egypt, Jordan, Morocco, Saudi Arabia, and Tunisia within the next few years. Some markets are also looking carefully at India's practice of permitting currency convertibility for certain stock and bond portfolios; the goal is to encourage investment by expatriate nationals while still limiting participation by foreigners. All this, market planners believe, will stimulate private-sector, equity-driven development, particularly in those emerging markets with a history of government-led, centralized development. But like the BSE, the Gulf-based exchanges see themselves as potentially more than Arab markets: Officials from Kuwait to the United Arab Emirates have pointed out that they are favorably located between Europe and Japan to be a key link in the 24-hour global market. One goal of a Gulf regional market, officials say, would thus be to solicit trade from large transnational and multinational corporations that are seeking round-the-clock availability of market facilities.

Cognitive Questions

1. Why would potential investors have an interest in small stock markets?
2. In what way can foreign investors generate change in these markets? Explain.
3. Why are Arab exchanges expected to outperform markets in the U.S., Europe, and Japan?
4. If this happens, what would be the consequences to the world? For the U.S.? For you and your family?
5. Why are Middle Eastern markets eager to attract international investments?
6. Why would nonMiddle Easterners invest in such markets? Would you invest in such markets? Why or why not?

Affective Questions

1. As in the case of Bahrain, should foreign investors be limited in their purchase of stock in Bahrain's companies? Why or why not?
2. If this practice prevails, should the U.S. and other Western countries respond in kind? Why or why not?
3. If globalization is the goal, is it fair for some countries or groups of countries to restrict investment by "foreign" nationals?

4. If you were given an opportunity to invest, would you invest in a domestic or in a foreign market?
5. Would you personally trust countries with growing stock markets to honor your investment? Why or why not?
6. Do you believe that interests in the developed, industrial regions dominate emerging stock markets? If this observation is accurate, is it fair?
7. If the developed countries control the developing countries, what could be done to make a fairer world?

Following up discussions on the affective concerns, questions calling for direct participation into world affairs are in order:

1. Knowing that there is great competition in this field, would you support the growth of emerging stock markets?
2. If you support this growth, what would you personally do to help the markets grow?
3. Would you support an international stock exchange center (SEC) which would assure the world that transactions will be done in an open manner? What strategies would you employ to realize this goal?
4. If you believe that groups and special interests in the developed countries control stock markets in the developing countries, what would you propose to do so that some measure of world equity is established? How would you go about proposing change strategies that could be effective? How would you marshal support for your position?
5. In order to accomplish your goal, what national or international agencies would you approach?
6. After you have answered all of these questions, list the specific actions you are presently taking.
7. What actions have been successful? Unsuccessful?
8. Would you change your strategies to ensure your success? Explain.

Example 3: The United Nations and Conflict among Nations

This lesson may begin by asking students to role-play the actions of the United Nations Security Council in sanctioning Iraq for refusing to allow U.S. citizens to be part of the inspection team of the Disarmament Commission in Iraq. This commission and its inspection teams were created by the UN to monitor the conditions in Iraq after the forced withdrawal of Iraqi troops from Kuwait.

Students are asked to assume the positions of both permanent and nonpermanent members of the Security Council and to debate the issue. A group of students are also asked to present the Iraqi position. All of the students are asked to read some background material, including newspaper accounts of the event. Such an account is given in the article "Unanimous Security Council Tightens the Vise on Iraq" by Barbara Crossette, (1997):

*Unanimous Security Council Tightens the Vise on Iraq**

United Nations—the Security Council, in a unanimous vote, made good Wednesday on its intention to impose new sanctions on Iraq, including banning foreign travel by Iraqi officials who do not cooperate with a UN disarmament commission. But Iraqi officials immediately said they would defy the demands, raising new questions about what will happen next.

Iraqi Deputy Prime Minister Tariq Aziz said in a statement in New York that the resolution was "unjust" and would be ignored.

"Iraq rejects and condemns the Security Council resolution and stresses that the resolution will not scare it," Aziz said in the statement, released at the United Nations by the Iraqi News Agency.

However, Bill Richardson, the U.S. representative at the United Nations, said, "The message has been clear."

He added: "The Security Council has been united. Iraq must comply or face consequences. We are not precluding any option, including the military option."

The Clinton administration and the British government take the view that the use of force is already authorized by existing UN resolutions. And they say that view is underlined by a provision in Wednesday's resolution calling for unspecified "further action" against Baghdad if President Saddam Hussein does not rescind an order to expel American weapons inspectors.

Russia has another opinion however. Sergey Lavrov, the Russian representative to the United Nations, said Wednesday that any proposed use of force would have to be approved by the Council. France and China agree. All three nations have a veto in the Council.

In addition, the Russians and Chinese both raised the possibility that the Council would have to look anew at Iraqi sanctions and the work of the disarmament commission.

In its resolution, the Security Council also condemned Iraq for threatening to shoot down U-2 surveillance planes, blocking inspections and hiding equipment during the current crisis and called Iraqi actions "a threat to international peace and security." President Clinton has said that the United States would view any attempt to shoot down a U-2 as an act of war.

In Baghdad, arms inspection monitors were again barred from entering sites they wanted to investigate because there were Americans on the team.

Aziz, who has been in New York arguing Iraq's case, did not ask to address the Security Council in Wednesday, after it became evident that all 15 council members supported the resolution.

While the United States and Britain did not get as strong a resolution as some Western officials may have initially preferred, the fact remains that the Iraqis have done considerably worse. A diplomatic gain made three weeks ago, when the Security Council was seriously divided over the travel ban, has been reversed, and Baghdad has suffered a diplomatic setback.

On October 23, China, France, Russia, Egypt and Kenya abstained from support of even a watered down resolution postponing consideration of the ban until April. That ban now takes immediate effect.

A list of Iraqis who will be prohibited from international travel will be drawn up by the Security Council Sanctions Committee dealing with Iraq, in consultation with the Special Commission and its chairman, Richard Butler, an Australian arms control expert. The list will be distributed to all UN member governments.

Iraqis on legitimate diplomatic missions will be exempt.

The resolution allows for the lifting of the ban if Butler reports to the Security Council that Iraq has given inspectors "immediate unconditional and unrestricted access to any and all areas, facilities, equipment, records and means of transportation which they wish to inspect."

Iraqi Foreign Minister Mohammed Seed al-Sahhaf responded to President Clinton's warning that Iraq remains a danger to the world, calling the comment "a sheer lie" by a superpower attempting to "absolve the already controversial integrity of its president."

U.S. military flights over Iraq have doubled since the latest crisis began, al-Sahhaf added during a Baghdad news conference carried by CNN-International. He repeats Iraq's warning that "Whenever we see it proper to shoot them, we will shoot them."

Reaching for explanations of why Iraq had lost its attempt to head off further sanctions, Sahhaf accused Washington of browbeating the Security Council and creating a "hysterical atmosphere at the United Nations."

(*Information from the Associated Press was used to supplement this report.*)

The skill objectives of this lesson fall under all three domains in the table of specifications (Figure 2.1) as well as under the substantive label, "2.1 Political World Subsystem." Students representing the countries involved in the dispute may be asked to prepare statements that respond to the following:

1. What is the issue at stake? (evaluative)
2. What is your position on the issue? (evaluative)
3. What are the grounds for your position? (evaluative)
4. What do you propose can be done to resolve the issue? (participatory)
5. What can be done to gain support for each representative's proposal? (participatory)
6. What are the likely consequences of acting on each proposal? (participatory)
7. What is the final vote by each representative and why? (participatory)

The use of role-playing strategies allows the class to immerse itself in the information surrounding an international controversy and to experience the challenges in formulating positions and acting on critical issues affecting the world community. After the class completes the exercise, students may be prompted to express their views publicly by writing student newspaper editorials; sending proposals to members of the UN Security Council; contacting local, national, or international newspaper and magazine editors; and using the Internet to communicate their positions and concerns with fellow students throughout the world.

It should be noted that while the examples here may be more appropriate for secondary school students, teachers can simplify the materials for students in the elementary school. Role-playing exercises, simulations, and games are certainly effective ways to involve elementary school students in issues involving the world community. The chapters that follow may provide several ideas to the teacher in composing scenarios on global issues and presenting them to their students through the various activities suggested in this chapter.

SUMMARY

This chapter discusses the development of a framework for implementing inquiry classroom strategies that aim at exploring global issues in the classroom. The strategy examples presented provide a context for students to understand how the world system and its subsystems operate and to form a consciousness that each student is part of the world community, known as the global village.

Through the use of the springboards in the examples, students engage in a full gamut of cognitive, affective, and participatory activities concerning global affairs. For example, they learn how to hypothesize about the consequences of unlimited population growth on the global environment. They also hypothesize on the effects of this growth on themselves and their families. As the students explore these issues, they begin to realize that whatever happens in any part of the world, even in seemingly isolated places, has repercussions for the entire world. Globalization, as the state of the world, is in full swing and affects everyone. Students who cannot develop the conceptual tools to understand and explain issues in their global environment may have difficulty coping with global issues later in life.

The examples in this chapter clearly show how teachers and their students can deal with attitudes and values relating to global issues. Explaining the state of the world is not enough. Students need to learn how to develop and reflect on their attitudes and values and how to arrive at defensible positions concerning world conflicts. One of the effects of inquiry into values for students might be a reduction of a feeling of xenophobia that some of them might have. All students now have the opportunity to have direct contact with global topics and issues. Knowledge of other peoples and cultures inescapably reduces any xenophobic attitudes students might have. To cope with their environment, students begin to develop global rather than provincial orientations toward it. They begin to develop affinities and empathy toward their fellow global citizens.

Explaining the world and effectively being part of it are important tasks. Beyond these tasks, however, students need to learn how to involve themselves directly in world affairs, such as how to engage in appropriate actions to attain their carefully analyzed objectives. Springboards used with students are followed by questions that seek to involve them in social and political participation. For example, students may learn how to observe the operations of the world's economic system and to identify key decisions that have an impact on them and their families. If these are unfair decisions, how can the decisions be changed? What do people gain and what do people lose if they take certain actions to offer input into such decisions? How do people obtain support to implement their plan? How do they act or carry out their decisions? How do they ensure their success?

Through the implementation of these instructional strategies, students will sharpen their cognitive, affective, and participatory skills concerning global issues. These strategies and the activities in which they engage help strengthen student self-concept and self-confidence. Students learn that they can control the world around them rather than being controlled by it. They develop a sense of world political and social efficacy, which means they understand how the world system operates and feel competent in changing it. With this type of experience, students may be self confident, successful, and optimistic about the future.

QUESTIONS FOR REFLECTION

1. This chapter presents the concept of globalization. How does this concept present itself in everyday life, such as in the foods we eat, in the cars we drive, and in the newspapers we read? Is this a worthwhile concept and area of study to be introduced in the classroom?

2. Teachers are usually asked to prepare educational objectives and lesson plans (at least for the coming week) before implementing them in the classroom. Given the objectives presented in this chapter, which ones would you select for implementation, and why? Prepare your own table of specifications.

3. If the sample of objectives presented in this chapter are not appropriate for your students, how would you go about developing your own objectives? What factors would you take into consideration in developing your own objectives?

4. Assuming you have developed a set of objectives on global studies which are appropriate for the level of students you have (elementary, middle, or high school students), decide which of the following you would select to implement your objectives:

    a. Thought-provoking materials (springboards), such as photos, articles, cartoons, textbooks, and materials obtained through such sources as Encarta Encyclopedia, Internet Explorer, and Netscape?

    b. Teaching methods or strategies, including lecture, inquiry-based discussion, role-playing, and games?

    c. Evaluation instruments, which could provide feedback to you and your students about whether or not objectives have been accomplished, such as, standardized tests, essays, reports, interviews, and anecdotal records?

5. Select a global issue of contemporary importance, such as ozone depletion or overpopulation, and develop a table of specifications to include objectives in the three domains: cognitive, affective, and participatory. Given the objectives you plan to emphasize, how would you go about integrating them in a lesson for a subject you are asked to teach (social studies, language arts, science, math, or foreign language)?

6. Assuming you have debated an important issue in class, such as global warming, what would you ask your students to do in order to practice their participatory skills? What would they have to do to reach the key decision makers whose actions relate to the issue? List the specific participatory acts in which your students would engage.

REFERENCES

Bloom, B. S., Englehart, M. D., Furst, E. J., Hill, W. H., & Krathwohl, D. R. (1956). *Taxonomy of educational objectives: Handbook I, Cognitive domain.* New York: McKay.

Crossette, B. (1997, November 13). Unanimous Security Council Tightens the Vise on Iraq. *The New York Times,* p. A6.

Featherstone, M., Lash, S., & Robertson, R. (Eds.). (1995). *Global Modernities.* London, England: Sage.

Green. C. P. (1992, May). The environment and population growth: Decade for action. *Population Reports, M*(10), 5, 9.

Harrow, A. J. (1972). *A taxonomy of the psychomotor domain.* New York: McKay.

Kauchak, D. P., & Eggen, P. D. (1998). *Learning and teaching: Research based methods* (3rd ed.). Boston: Allyn & Bacon.

Krathwohl, D. R., Bloom, B. S., & Masia, B. B. (1964). *Taxonomy of educational objectives: Handbook II, Affective domain.* New York: McKay.

Martin, J. (1996, January/February). Taking stock. *Aramco World, 47*(1), 2–11.

Massialas, B. G., & Hurst, J. B. (1978). *Social studies in a new era: The elementary school as a laboratory.* New York: Longman.

United Nations. (1994, September 9). *Program of Action of the United Nations.* International Conference on Population and Development, Cairo, Egypt.

Worthen, B. R., Borg, W. R., & White, K. R. (1993). *Measurement and evaluation in the schools.* New York: Longman.

3

CURRICULUM IN
GLOBAL EDUCATION

Major Points

- Teachers need to be aware of the attitudes toward global education that are present in the schools and communities where they teach.
- Support for global education can vary along a local-to-global continuum as well as along a human-to-material scale.
- The Hanvey, Kniep, and Merryfield and White models of implementing global education all place significant emphasis on critical thinking and understanding the perspectives of other people and nations.
- The infusion approach of implementing a global education curriculum has significant advantages over the separate unit and course approach.
- A thorough global education curriculum emphasizes that heterogeneity, not homogeneity, is present in the populations of most nations.
- The pedagogy for teaching global education should involve the cognitive, affective, and participatory domains.
- The hidden curriculum in U.S. schools promotes competition, the pleasing of authorities, and academic passivity.
- Textual representation global education issues can be examined by comparing treatment of issues in two or more texts.

- Discussing some controversial issues is a necessary component of a sound global education curriculum. The degree of controversy surrounding an issue is often determined by the personal stake individuals have in the topic.
- The academic freedom of teachers requires that information presented in class must be factually correct, germane to the subject, and within the intellectual maturity of learners to understand.
- Research findings indicate that U.S. students need to increase their understanding of global issues and events.

A curriculum, which is a running sequence of learning events, represents significant perspectives and knowledge in a society selected for transmission to the next generation. By examining curricular content, an observer can learn a great deal about a society's values, perspectives, and identity.

Before setting out to teach a global education curriculum, educators need to be aware of the attitudinal dimensions of the society in which global education will occur. Is the general predisposition toward global issues and interdependence similar in Amsterdam, Netherlands, or Austin, Texas? Does it matter if you teach in Alexandria, Virginia, or Alexandria, Egypt? The following graphic provides one way of analyzing societal attitudes that will have a strong bearing on global education.

1. *Human–Global Emphasis:* Persons with this orientation will likely support global education and stress its importance as a vehicle for improving human conditions throughout the globe. Documents such as The Universal Declaration of Human Rights are of paramount importance for persons with this perspective.
2. *Human–Local Emphasis:* This orientation stresses solving problems at home before becoming concerned with issues abroad. Reducing a nation's international presence and commitments can support domestic social policies.
3. *Material–Local Emphasis:* This view focuses on having education prepare students to fit particular niches in a nation's economy. It also favors protectionist policies that would isolate, as much as possible, a nation's economy from trends in the world's economy.
4. *Material–Global Emphasis:* This position supports global literacy and foreign language skills, because they make a nation's busi-

ness more internationally competitive. However, this view would look at human rights abuses or child labor problems as primarily the concern of the nation where these problems occur.

While it can certainly be argued that no one fits entirely into one quadrant of Figure 3.1 (persons can have overlapping identifications), the figure is useful in analyzing the variety of reactions likely to be found among students and parents exposed to global education curricula.

Students who come from homes which stress human–local or material–local views may not see the relevance of studying human rights abuses stemming from a civil war in Bosnia or of examining the plight of the Kurds driven into Turkey by Iraq shortly after the end of the Gulf War. The question that is often asked by students and their parents who share this view is one regarding relevance: "How does this affect us at home?" A teacher presenting this material in an international human rights lesson could point out that both situations, directly or indirectly, involved U.S. troops. Thus, seemingly remote international issues can touch even the most isolated community.

Support for global education can also vary in both strength and direction. A local chamber of commerce may support curricular elements that teach students to recognize cultural differences in other nations and provide the students with second language competency. These are, after all, key ingredients for anyone doing business

FIGURE 3.1   Attitudes toward Global Education

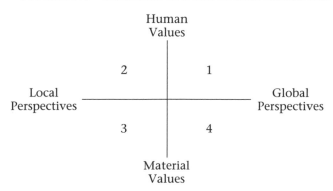

across national boundaries. The same chamber of commerce may question spending significant time studying international human rights issues, or it may support global education with both human and economic dimensions.

In structuring and teaching a global education curriculum, teachers and administrators need to take the pulse of their communities. Do members of the community view global education as inherently hostile to the nation and thus unpatriotic? Do they believe that a curriculum stressing the global interconnections of environment, immigration, and human rights issues undermines community values?

If these views are present, it is important to stress before instruction occurs that global education content does not diminish national identity. The study of issues abroad supports the study of similar issues at home.

ORGANIZING A GLOBAL EDUCATION CURRICULUM

What should be included in a well-planned education for global understanding? What perspectives are imperative for educators to share with students? The answers to these questions may appear overwhelming at first glance. However, a number of guidelines have been developed to help provide structure to this task.

Willard Kniep (1989) devised a model for global education that stresses the study of five concepts in the curriculum: interdependence, change, conflict, scarcity, and culture. In addition to these concepts, Kniep organized his global education curriculum around four other essential areas: systems, human values, problems, and global history. A global education curriculum that covers all of Kniep's key concepts and dimensions would be a thorough one.

Another model through which to organize a global education curriculum was developed by Robert Hanvey. This model consists of the following five dimensions:

1. *Perspective Consciousness:* An awareness of and appreciation for other images of the world, and recognition that others have views of the world that are profoundly different from one's own.

2. *State-of-the-Planet Awareness:* An in-depth understanding of prevailing global issues, events, and conditions.
3. *Cross-Cultural Awareness:* A general understanding of the defining characteristic of world cultures with an emphasis on understanding differences and similarities.
4. *Knowledge of Global Dynamics:* Consciousness of global change, familiarity with the nature of systems, and an introduction to the complex international system in which state and nonstate actors are linked in a variety of issues areas.
5. *Awareness of Human Choices:* A review of strategies for action on issues in local, national, and international settings (Tye & Tye, 1992, pp. 86–87).

Teachers attempting to apply the criteria of the Hanvey model to their instruction of global issues must have a broad base of information on global topics and a willingness to expose students to varied perspectives.

Merryfield and White (1996, p. 179) propose that in selecting global issues for social studies, the following areas be examined: political issues, cultural–social issues, development issues, economic issues, and environmental issues. In addition to citing numerous categories within each set of issues, Merryfield and White also stress the presentation of multiple perspectives on issues and the interconnectedness of the world.

How can far-reaching standards such as the Hanvey, Kniep, and Merryfield and White models be implemented in today's schools? What are the best mechanisms to achieve these goals?

One often used approach is the creation of a separate unit or a separate course to provide global perspectives and information. One advantage of this approach is its relatively simple implementation. An elementary teacher could research world issues, trends, and statistics. Then this teacher could present the information within a specified period of time (one or two weeks) and return to the standard curriculum. At the middle or high school level, a course on global issues would be offered typically as an elective course. This approach would involve special preparation by one or two teachers and not affect the entire faculty.

The disadvantages of the separate unit or course approach are varied. Students may or may not see the connections between the global knowledge presented as a separate unit or course and the rest of the curriculum. Whatever material is presented in separate units or courses does not reach all students, and this suggests that global information does not have the same legitimacy as the content in the required curriculum. The ease of implementation of the separate unit or course approach must be weighed against its inherent disadvantages. It can be argued that it is better to present global issues, information, and perspectives separately than not at all. If educators use the separate unit or course approach, they should view it as a stepping stone toward a curriculum in which global perspectives have a significant and natural integration with all academic content.

More comprehensive than the separate unit or course method is the infusion approach. Here, global information, readings, and perspectives are incorporated into the lesson plans of the core curriculum. The advantages of the infusion approach are that (1) global material and perspectives have a clear connection with material in the discipline, because the two are being taught together, (2) an infusion approach would affect the core curriculum and reach all students, and (3) students would be able to make the global connection across disciplines, because the global dimension was being emphasized in all subjects.

The infusion approach also has the advantage that it can be used to meet existing curricular guidelines without requiring additional classroom time. Global education content can be woven into the language arts and writing curriculum to meet objectives that improve reading and writing. In addition, students can be learning information about other nations and cultures while improving their English language skills.

Similarly, global information can be incorporated into mathematics (history of mathematics), science (scientific research and contributions from other nations), and social studies (world cultures and geography, world history, and comparative political systems). Infusing global content into the curriculum is not a contrived task, since nearly every subject has significant and legitimate international dimensions.

One of the difficulties in implementing the infusion approach to a global education curriculum is that some teachers may not have the necessary global information to apply to their teaching without significant additional training. Educators who teach outside the social studies field may view infusing global perspectives as solely the responsibility of their social studies colleagues. Some teachers could complain, "If we have taught without a significant global emphasis for two decades, why must we change now?" Other educators may tacitly agree to provide a global emphasis in the curriculum but implement it by sponsoring an international dinner or requiring students to just memorize important capital cities of the world. Clearly, these last approaches would not meet the high standards suggested by Hanvey, Kniep, and Merryfield and White.

SELECTING CONTENT FOR THE GLOBAL EDUCATION CURRICULUM

Teachers may select a wide variety of content to teach under the heading of global education. In order to meet the criteria set forth in global education models described earlier in this chapter, it is imperative that the content selected for a global education curriculum encourages students to engage in activities ranging from factual recall to critical thinking and comparative analysis.

A sound global education curriculum must contain both mainstream and transformative academic knowledge (defined in Chapter 1). The latter is particularly useful for encouraging students to engage in higher-order thinking. Transformative academic knowledge should be presented with two caveats in mind. First, information selected should be well researched and documented. Next, teachers should keep in mind the maturity and cognitive sophistication of students.

In teaching about slavery in the Americas, upper elementary teachers who first introduce the topic to students can point out that a variety of European nations engaged in the trans-Atlantic slave trade. They should mention the need for additional labor (relative to land) in both North and South America. They could also point out the huge profits in the slave trade as well as the economic value of labor slaves provided.

There were many aspects of the trans-Atlantic and domestic slave trade that were terribly inhumane. Examples such as details of living conditions on slave ships, the "breaking" of slaves on Caribbean islands before being shipped to the United States, and the division of slave families by selling away members, are inappropriate for elementary students. They should be shared with students when they have reached an appropriate level of mental maturation (middle or high school, depending on the topic).

When students in the United States study the topic of slavery, this issue is presented largely in a domestic context. How many high school seniors could answer questions such as, "Contrast the similarities and differences of slavery in the United States, islands of the Caribbean, and Brazil?" or "Explain the impact of centuries of the trans-Atlantic slave trade on the African regions from which slaves were obtained?"

Questions of this nature, along with the necessary information to answer them, would move the presentation of slavery largely from a national context to a global one. Students who could analyze the issues of slavery in a global context would have a profound understanding of the topic.

Another essential element in selecting content for a global education curriculum is the realization that heterogeneity, not homogeneity, is generally the rule in the world. A major Western society such as Spain may be presented to students as a historical colonial power. Its people may be perceived by most students in the United States as simply Spanish: dark complected, dark haired, and Spanish speaking. Many Spaniards fit this description, while many do not. Large numbers of Basques, Galicians, and Catalans speak Spanish as a second language. Millions of people in northern Spain are of Celtic origin and more closely resemble the populations of England or Ireland than their fellow Spaniards in southern Spain.

When minimal information is presented on other nations (whether through omission or commission), an impression of homogeneity in that nation's population is left with students. This notion of a homogeneous people often remains, although the nation's population is actually quite diverse.

The selection of content for a global education curriculum is correlated with pedagogy that is likely to be employed. Teachers who select only mainstream academic knowledge (capital cities of Europe or major exports of Central American nations) are unlikely to choose teaching methods that engender critical thinking and analysis. Some factual content is necessary to understand complex global issues, but teaching facts exclusively can lend itself to a fill-in-the-blank notion of education and evaluation.

Conversely, transformative knowledge is more likely to promote higher-order or critical thinking among students. A well-planned global education curriculum needs elements of mainstream academic and transformational knowledge about global topics in order to be effective.

PEDAGOGY FOR GLOBAL EDUCATION

The teaching methods selected to convey global topics or issues should allow students experiences at the cognitive, affective, and participatory levels. In the cognitive realm, information should be presented along with concepts, build on concepts and information presented earlier in the curriculum, and provide for critical thinking. In the affective and participatory realms, learning activities should allow students to understand global issues from the perspectives of others, develop empathy for other human groups, and engage in activities that develop a sense of efficacy in students regarding global issues.

An example of global education curriculum activities built around the theme of immigration follows:

Primary (Grades 1–3)

1. Key terms/ideas

   a. Nation
   b. Modes of transportation
   c. Better life
   d. Families

2. Activities

   a. Identify on a map the continents where immigrants to the United States began their journeys. (cognitive)
   b. Ask students to question their parents and grandparents about the national origins of their families. (participatory)
   c. Invite immigrant children to speak to the class about how they felt about their first year of life in the United States. (affective)

   d. Identify the major modes of transportation used by immigrants in different eras. (cognitive)
   e. Ask students to look at photographs of persons from each continent. Then ask them to point out any similarities and differences they see. (cognitive)

Upper Elementary (Grades 4–5)

1. Key terms/ideas

   a. Patterns of movement
   b. Economic–political conditions
   c. Cultural groups
   d. Family reunification

2. Activities

   a. Ask students to read letters from nineteenth century immigrants to relatives in their home countries, describing life in the United States. (cognitive, affective)
   b. Have students interview immigrants in their communities and ask them why they immigrated to the United States. (participatory)
   c. Ask students to identify on a map where each generation of their families lived until the points reach some area outside of the United States. (The family trees of Native American students will likely remain in North America.) (cognitive)
   d. Interview immigrants who have tried to bring relatives to join them in the United States and ask them what the rules are governing the entry of relatives. (participatory, cognitive)
   e. Ask students to write to the United Nations in New York City asking for information on the nations that accept the most immigrants and the nations that provide the most emigrants. (participatory, cognitive)

Middle School (Grades 6–8)

1. Key terms/ideas

   a. Immigration policy
   b. Emigration
   c. Refugee

    d. Cultural assimilation

    e. Cultural diversity

2. Activities

    a. Have students draft a short questionnaire to measure attitudes toward immigrants. Administer the questionnaire to persons born inside and outside of the United States. Compare the results of the two samples. (participatory)

    b. Ask students to write to their representatives or senators in Washington, D.C., asking for a description of the laws that constitute current immigration policy. After small group and class discussion of the responses, ask students to again write to their representatives and senators expressing their views on this issue. (participatory, cognitive)

    c. Have students create bar graphs depicting immigration to the United States for each decade of the twentieth century. Ask other students to create similar graphs illustrating emigration. The Department of Immigration and Naturalization within the Department of Justice would be a good source for the raw data. (cognitive)

    d. Contact the United Nations Commission on Refugees in New York City to receive current data on refugee movement. Use this data to chart refugee patterns on a map of the world. (cognitive)

    e. Ask someone who fled their nation under duress to describe that experience to your students. (affective)

High School (Grades 9–12)

1. Key terms/ideas

    a. Political asylum

    b. National origin quotas

    c. Economic integration

    d. Nativism

    e. Immigration policy in other nations

    f. Proportion of foreign born population in various nations.

2. Activities

    a. Ask students to work in pairs. One member of the pair will contact a nation's embassy in Washington, D.C. and ask for information regarding that nation's immigration policy and proportion of foreign born population. The second member will ask the same information from the Department of Foreign Affairs in that nation's capital. After all responses are received, compare the two sources of information. (participatory, cognitive)

b. Using the data gained in the previous activity, create a chart which ranks nations by the proportion of foreign born population. After discussing the information on the immigration policy of various nations, ask students to vote and place nations in order from the most open to the most restrictive in terms of immigration policy. (cognitive)

c. Ask students to research the Immigration Acts of 1917, 1921, 1924, and 1965. What role did the nationality of immigrants play in the policies established by the United States in each law? Did nativism play a role in any of this legislation? If so, why? If not, why not? (cognitive)

d. About 33% of the Nobel Prize winners from the United States have been foreign born. However, the proportion of foreign born U.S. citizens during the period the Nobel Prize has been awarded is less than 15%. What does this indicate about the immigrant population? Is this fact well known? Why or why not? (cognitive)

e. In small groups, students should prepare questionnaires for the public concerning immigration. Questions should concern facts about immigration and attitudes toward immigrants. After administering the questionnaires, student groups should compile their data. Is there a relationship between persons who have more or less knowledge about immigration and have more or less favorable attitudes toward immigrants? If so, what is the relationship? Ask student groups to prepare graphs and charts to illustrate their findings. (cognitive, participatory, affective)

f. If students have e-mail access, contact groups of similar-age students in other nations. Using the questionnaire developed in the previous activity, ask students in other nations to conduct the questionnaire and e-mail their results to you. Compare the data samples across nations to determine which populations had the greatest knowledge of immigrants in their societies and the most or least favorable attitudes toward immigrants. (cognitive, affective, participatory)

The examples of important ideas and activities described suggest that topics generally taught in the domestic context can easily be presented in a global one. Students should engage in learning activities that range from the assimilation of new information on global issues to critical thinking and analysis of these topics. Finally, activities should be used that present students with opportunities to learn at the cognitive, affective, and participatory levels.

THE HIDDEN CURRICULUM

The hidden curriculum is a term that has been used to describe the conformity that schools demand from students. Among the values promoted by the hidden curriculum are teacher-pleasing, academic competition, and individualism, as well as passivity and conformity to school rules. These values are sometimes subtly promoted by school practices and rewards. Students who do not conform to these values often find themselves facing personal or academic difficulties.

There is evidence that social studies classes in working-class schools are taught in a manner that stresses the reproduction of facts rather than critical thinking. Conversely, in affluent schools the students are more frequently asked to engage in divergent thinking and develop creative ideas or solutions (Anyon, 1980).

The patterns of instruction suggested by the hidden curriculum give students that are more affluent greater opportunities in schools. These are the opportunities to learn the principles needed to be effective national and global citizens. Massialas (1996, p. 71) notes that "cultural reproduction through the hidden curriculum is complete and realized in American schools. Social studies, more than any other subject, is full of hidden messages that are constantly conveyed to the students."

A useful tool for working with the hidden curriculum in the study of global education is to have students examine how two or more textbooks describe the same global issue or event. After a careful comparison of the language of the texts, a teacher could pose the following questions:

1. Are there any important facts presented in one text and not in the other?
2. Do the authors approach this issue or event from a neutral perspective? Why or why not?
3. If you feel the authors have a position or philosophy regarding this topic, what is it and why do they feel this way?
4. Is there any pertinent information or perspective that the authors might have included to give you a better understanding of the topic? If so, what?
5. If anything is lacking from the narratives on the same topic in these texts, why do you think it is missing?

These questions place the student in the role of an "investigator" on global issues rather than being simply a passive recipient of information. Far too often, students take the view that if it is in writing, "it is chiseled in marble." Raising questions regarding varying interpretations of facts by authors places the student in the role of an active participant and gives education a liberating quality.

CONTROVERSIAL ISSUES AND GLOBAL EDUCATION

Techniques like these and others that generate critical thinking need to be employed particularly with students from lower socioeconomic class settings, because these students generally have the least exposure to critical thinking in school. However, all students can benefit from increasing the proportion of class time spent on critical thinking, and global education is an excellent vehicle through which to achieve this.

Teaching controversial issues is something that teachers of global education must occasionally do if their teaching is going to meet the standards of the Hanvey, Kniep, or Merryfield and White models.

A pertinent question to raise at this point is, "What constitutes a controversial issue?" Not all topics on which there are differences of opinion are controversial. Raising the question, "Does Sweden or Norway provide more humanitarian aid to needy nations?" could generate research on this topic as well as different opinions from students. The research should indicate the percentage of gross national product devoted to humanitarian aid in *krone* or dollars and the amount of humanitarian aid per capita. Students could discuss which measures are most accurate in order to answer the question.

Whatever the conclusion (although there may be differences of opinion), this is not a controversial issue because most students don't feel they have a personal stake in the outcome. By substituting the United States for Sweden and making the question a comparison of Norway with the United States, the potential for controversy increases. Many students will want the research to indicate that the United States is the more generous nation in terms of humanitarian aid, since they are citizens of the United States; they have a personal stake in the issue. After researching this issue, students could discuss whether total dollars contributed per year in humanitarian aid or the proportion of gross national product devoted to humanitarian aid is the more accurate measure. The former statistic favors the larger nation: the United States. The latter statistic favors Norway. Whatever the outcome of the discussion, this comparison is likely to be more controversial than the Sweden and Norway analysis because of the personal stake held by some students.

Many curricular topics have come under scrutiny in U.S. schools. Among these have been global education, critical thinking, decision making, values education, the promotion of a positive view of the United Nations, and international studies (Jenkinson, 1990). Academic freedom is a value that has long been cherished in U.S. education. However, attempts at censorship have sometimes followed the teaching of controversial issues in schools. An important question to raise at this juncture is, "What should be protected by academic freedom and what should not?"

Academic freedom should apply to material that is presented by an educator teaching within an area of expertise that is germane to the subject(s) taught. There are two important caveats to remember: (1) the material should be well researched, factually correct, and presented in a balanced manner, and (2) the material should be age appropriate and within the cognitive sophistication of the learners. Thus, a discussion of Pol Pot's genocide of over one million Cambodians, although factually correct, would violate the second standard with a third grade class. The same topic, however, would be perfectly appropriate for high school juniors or seniors.

Jack Nelson provides the following important reminder about the need to teach controversial issues in democratic societies:

In fact, every nation provides forms of nationalistic education in its schools. Where nationalistic education undermines democratic education is where the emphasis on patriotic chauvinism requires contorting knowledge to hide the defects each nation has, or to give an unnecessarily negative portrayal of counternational ideas. These efforts deny critical thinking, a basic condition for open democracy. (Nelson, 1996, p. 391)

Any attempt to present global issues and events with the avoidance of controversy as a primary goal provides students with a caricature of the truth. When this is done (and it is not an uncommon occurrence), it happens because an educator wishes to play it safe or perhaps because the educator does not feel comfortable handling the questions that are likely to be generated by providing a complete (and more controversial) portrayal. However, playing it safe in this manner carries its own risks. Some students, or their parents, may regard a safe but myopic presentation as inadequate and bring the issue to the teacher's attention. If students do this during class, it could prove to be potentially embarrassing for the teacher. Advance notification of topics that will be studied is a good way to reduce any concerns of parents. However, if parents complain, it is easier for teachers to provide documentation to support teaching a controversial issue than to justify presenting a limited or incomplete lesson.

In the final analysis, there is no risk-free way to teach. With regard to controversial issues in global education or other subjects, the question is, "Which risks do educators wish to run?" It is intellectually more defensible to run the risk inherent in teaching controversial issues than to face the risks in the omission of controversial topics. However, each educator must respond to this question individually. Certainly, the more content and global education background educators possess, the more comfortable they feel discussing the controversial elements of global issues.

CLASSROOM CLIMATE AND ATTITUDES TOWARD GLOBAL EDUCATION

A study titled "Survey of Global Awareness" was sponsored by the Educational Testing Service and surveyed approximately 1,500 students in nine states. The study found that not all global education programs were successful. The most successful programs were aimed at advanced students and provided additional training about global issues for teachers. The least successful global education programs were newly created, but traditional, courses that focused on one area or region (Torney-Purta in Zevin, 1992, p. 246).

Clearly, having teachers who are well grounded in global issues is important. However, the climate that pervades the classroom and the comfort level students feel in exploring global and/or controversial issues are of paramount importance. One researcher found that an issues-oriented global curriculum, along with a classroom atmosphere that encouraged frank and open discussion, promoted interest and concern about global issues (Blankenship, 1990).

Other researchers have found that more effective teaching strategies, such as using divergent questions and giving students conflicting sources of information to analyze, encourage tolerance for dissent. Students who felt free to voice opinions different from the teacher's were likely to have more global information and greater interest in global issues (Torney-Purta & Lansdale, 1986). A study conducted in Michigan high schools found that global education courses influenced global attitudes only if students felt comfortable in expressing their views (Yocum, 1989). The findings in these studies collectively suggest that a classroom where the teacher conveys (however tacitly) a "correct" view for students to hold will not be an effective forum for global education. Students who examine global issues in an atmosphere of free and open inquiry may also reduce their stereotyping of other cultures.

It is particularly important when studying issues involving the United States and other nations that students are asked to examine the issues from the perspective of each nation. This type of analysis is critical to combat high levels of provincialism found among some students. Goodlad (1984) found that most social studies programs offered little global content, and more than half of the students surveyed felt that foreign countries and their ideas were dangerous to U.S. government. In contrast, Tucker (1983) surveyed a group of teachers in the Dade County (Miami, Florida) public schools and found that 90% felt global education was an important part of the social studies.

It is evident that classroom climate plays an important role in effective global education. A positive classroom climate—welcoming inquiry and with a teacher knowledgeable on global issues and comfortable discussing them—is ideal for effective global education.

The priority given to the role of global education in the curriculum can be determined by answering the question, "What level of international knowledge and literacy do we expect from U.S. students?" Most U.S. educators place significant value on having students who understand global issues. However, a study comparing the views of Swedish and American educators found that Swedish teachers were more globally oriented than their U.S. counterparts. Teachers in the U.S. sample gave little attention to the economic interconnectedness of peoples or to the disparities among countries in the production and consumption of necessities (Mahan & Stachowski, 1990, pp. 56–58).

Another study of 3,000 college students compared international knowledge and attitudes found among community college sophomores, university freshmen, and university seniors. From 101 questions asked, the average scores were (1) university freshmen, 41.9; (2) community college sophomores, 40.5; and (3) university seniors, 50.5. The researchers concluded that these scores represented a considerable lack of global knowledge (Council on Learning, 1981, p. 4). The entire sample consistently rated malnutrition, racial and religious conflict, and denial of basic human rights as issues in which they had little interest, knew little about, or felt had little importance. Finally, the study found that education majors, the teachers of tomorrow, had the lowest scores on the global knowledge test (Council on Learning, 1981, pp. 38–39).

These findings, among others, suggest that a greater emphasis on global education is warranted in the schools, colleges, and universities of the United States. Much has been written in the past two decades to facilitate the incorporation of global education into daily curricular practice. Ultimately, it is the attitudes of teachers and their willingness to embrace global education and expand their knowledge of global issues that will determine the effectiveness of any global education curriculum.

SUMMARY

Teachers of global education must be aware of the attitudes in their schools and communities. Some communities are highly supportive of teachers who emphasize global issues and literacy. There are other communities that have perceived global education efforts as detracting from a national focus in the curriculum and, therefore, have criticized global education.

Some of the major curriculum theorists in global education (Hanvey, Kniep, Merryfield and White) have emphasized that a sound global education curriculum is much more than knowing facts about the world. Students need to understand the perspectives of other people and nations as well as the interconnectedness of global issues. Academic content selected for a global education curriculum should include mainstream and transformative academic knowledge. Transformative academic knowledge is particularly useful, because it challenges traditional perspectives and encourages critical thinking.

The pedagogy employed in a global education curriculum should introduce new information in ways that illustrate concepts students already understand. The difficulty level of concepts and the complexity of new information should increase as the learner matures. It is also important that the global education curriculum engages students at the cognitive, affective, and participatory levels.

Teachers of global education need to be aware that their efforts must compete with the influences of the hidden curriculum. These influences do not support cooperative learning, challenging questions raised by students, or divergent thinking. In addition, an appropriate global education curriculum requires teachers and students to discuss many controversial issues. For these discussions to be effective, they must be conducted in an atmosphere of free and open inquiry. Academic freedom must cover not only the teacher's ability to teach, but the ability of students to question curricular issues. When this open atmosphere is present, global education can have a positive impact on students' knowledge and attitudes toward global issues. If this atmosphere of open inquiry is missing, global education has little or no influence on students' attitudes toward global matters.

Most research findings suggest that students in the United States need to improve their knowledge of and concern for global issues. How well this challenge is met in the future will be determined by the emphasis placed on global education by teachers, communities, and the nation.

QUESTIONS FOR REFLECTION

1. In view of this chapter's description of possible community attitudes toward global education, what are some methods that teachers could employ to determine exactly what the attitudes are in their schools and communities on this topic?

2. Identify three factors common to the Hanvey, Kniep, and Merryfield and White models of global education. How do these three factors enhance the understanding of global topics?

3. Explain the advantages and disadvantages of the infusion and separate course and unit approaches to implementing global education. Which approach is the easiest to implement? Which has the most significant impact on students?

4. Exemplary pedagogy should involve students at the cognitive, affective, and participatory levels. In your experience as an elementary and secondary student, which level(s), has your education emphasized? If you have had minimal experience with some level(s), why do you think that is so?

5. Global education must be implemented within a school culture influenced by the hidden curriculum. Are global education and the hidden curriculum complementary? Why or why not?

6. What is the essential element of issues that make them controversial? Are issues that are controversial to some, necessarily controversial to all?

7. What are some of the responsibilities teachers should observe when using their academic freedom to teach? What happens to global education if teachers of global education fail to meet the responsibilities of academic freedom?

8. It has been stated that the lack of awareness of global issues by students in the United States is influenced by the fact that the United States is an "island continent" separated by large oceans from most other regions of the world. Do you agree or disagree with this statement? Please explain why you feel this way.

9. Global education has been criticized by some as taking away from nationalism and a national emphasis in the curriculum. Do you agree or disagree with this statement? Why or why not?

REFERENCES

Anyon, J. (1980). Social class and the hidden curriculum at work. *Journal of Education, 162,* 67–92.

Blankenship, G. (1990). Classroom climate, global knowledge, global attitudes, political attitudes. *Theory and Research in Social Education, 18,* 363–384.

Council on Learning. (1981). *What college students know and believe about their world.* New Rochelle, NY: Change Magazine Press.

Goodlad, J. (1984). *A place called school: Prospects for the future.* New York: McGraw-Hill.

Jenkinson, E. (1990). Child abuse in the hate factory. In A. Ochoa (Ed.), *Academic freedom to teach and learn.* Washington, DC: National Education Association.

Kniep, W. M. (1989). Social studies within a global education. *Social Education, 53*(6), 385, 399–403.

Mahan, J., & Stachowski, L. (1990). The many values of international teaching and study experiences for teacher education majors. In J. L. Easterly (Ed.), *Promoting global teacher education* (pp. 15–24). Reston, VA: Association of Teacher Educators.

Massialas, B. G. (1996). The hidden curriculum and social studies. In B. G. Massialas & R. Allen (Eds.), *Crucial issues in teaching social studies K–12.* Belmont, CA: Wadsworth.

Merryfleld, M. M., & White, C. S. (1996). Issues centered global education. In R. Evans & D. W. Saxs (Eds.), *Handbook on teaching social studies: NCSS bulletin 93* (pp. 177–187). Washington, DC: National Council for the Social Studies.

Nelson, J. (1996). Academic freedom. In B. G. Massialas & R. Allen (Eds.), *Crucial issues in teaching social studies K-12.* Belmont, CA: Wadsworth.

Torney-Purta, J., & Lansdale, D. (1986, April). Classroom Climate and process in international studies: Qualitative and quantitative evidence from the American schools and the World Project, Stanford, and the School Study. Paper presented at the annual meeting of the American Educational Research Association, San Francisco.

Tucker, J. L. (1983). Teacher attitudes toward global education: A report from Dade County. *Education Research Quarterly, 8*(1), 65–77.

Tye, B., & Tye, K. (1992). *Global education: A study for school change.* Albany, NY: State University of New York.

Yocum, M. J. (1989). An investigation of the effects of a global education curriculum on the attitudes of high school students (Doctoral dissertation, Michigan State University, 1989). *Dissertation Abstracts International, 50,* 620A.

Zevin, J. (1992). *Social Studies for the twenty-first century.* New York: Longman.

4

GLOBAL ISSUES: HUMAN RIGHTS, POPULATION, AND REFUGEES

Major Points

- Issues of human rights, population, and refugees can be used to teach global interdependence and global responsibility.
- Human rights are the cornerstone of building a civil global society.
- The human rights enjoyed by women differ significantly across nations.
- A basic economic foundation is necessary for persons to have the opportunity for human rights.
- Overpopulation is an issue of global concern.
- Demographic Transition Theory explains the stages followed by population growth.
- Programs to address population growth have been developed by nations as well as international organizations.
- The world's refugees are particularly prone to persecution in their host nations.
- Migrations of populations are most often caused by political, economic, and environmental reasons, as well as by ethnic tensions.

The authors wish to acknowledge the assistance of Victoria Samaras Polentas with the preparation of this chapter.

"The salvation of mankind lies only in making everything the concern of all," said Alexander Soltzhenitsyn (Bartlett, 1980, p. 895). Since the beginning of time, there has been an interdependence among people for survival. As communities moved from subsistence farming to producing products to sell and trade, their needs changed. For example, the weaver, no longer producing food, depended upon the farmer for food; the farmer, in turn, depended upon the weaver for clothing. The Industrial Revolution and the social changes it caused in societies increased people's interdependence. More recently, technological advances such as the Internet and telecommunication systems have brought interaction on a global scale to the average U.S. citizen.

Schools must explain the concept of global interdependence to students. How can this concept be explained in simple terms so that all can understand? For most, simple concrete examples such as food and clothing products can be used to illustrate the global market and global trade as well as to introduce the concept of economic interdependence. U.S. students of all ages understand that toys, televisions, radios, and cars made in other countries are available to them here in the United States. The question, "What if Japan stopped trade with the U.S.?" can initiate critical thinking and discussion as students make assumptions about the consequences of such a phenomenon and realize its impact.

The purpose of global education, however, is not merely to introduce and illustrate interdependence, but to generate a sense of global responsibility in students. Therefore, a teacher could use issues to teach both global interdependence and global responsibility. The issues teachers select should be connected and woven into a curricular framework from a vast array of scholarly sources on global topics. The issues ought to be important, relevant, and related to the everyday lives of U.S. citizens. Consider the following issues:

1. *Social Change:* Today, social change is taking place in the United States and in the world at a faster pace than at any other time in history. This is a world in transition.
2. *Environmental Change:* Issues involving pollution, radiation, global warming, and government involvement in medical research are of concern to the world's citizens.

3. *Population Issues:* Technological advances have led to significant breakthroughs in human fertility. In the developing world, the relationship of population to food supply is of constant concern.
4. *Natural and Human Resources:* Increase in population and the depletion of natural resources are concerns facing U.S. Citizens and the world. Developing human resources to the fullest is also a major concern. Providing properly trained people to keep up with rapid technological change is a challenge facing many nations.
5. *Development and Education Issues:* Students in developed nations, such as the United States, need to understand issues in developing nations from the perspective of citizens of those nations. Problems that seem relatively simple in developed nations are often quite complex in developing nations.
6. *War, Violence, and Peace Issues:* Wars throughout the world have a direct impact on the economy of the United States. The bipolar division of the world between the Soviet Union and the United States has been changed. Contemporary conflicts tend to center on ethnic and/or religious divisions and often defy easy categorizations.
7. *Human Rights Issues:* The rights of women to be free from sexual harassment and to receive equal pay for equal work are of great concern to U.S. citizens. The status of homosexuals in the U.S. military has undergone significant redefinition.

Global interdependence and responsibility in U.S. schools can be illustrated by using issues as a focus. As Dr. Martin Luther King, Jr. so aptly stated,

> Before you finish eating breakfast this morning, you've depended on more than half the world. This is the way our Universe is structured.... We aren't going to have peace on earth until we recognize this basic fact of the interrelated structure of all reality. (Bartlett, 1980, p. 110)

The issues teachers select ought to present students with a significant challenge. In addition, the issues should pertain to humanity's concern for today and tomorrow. It can be argued that there is no "correct" answer to the issues presented. However, educators should still explore these topics in order to prepare students for the twenty-first century. This chapter and the chapters that follow will present an assortment of issues of global importance.

HUMAN RIGHTS

It is imperative for the educational community to unite and work toward incorporating the study of human rights as an integral part of the core curriculum. Respect for human rights contributes to building an equitable and more civil global society. On a global scale, human rights are an extension of a process strongly endorsed by the United States Constitution and its Bill of Rights, as well as the English Bill of Rights (see Figure 4.1) and the French Declaration of the Rights of Man and Citizen (see Figure 4.2). Human rights represent foundations of global interdependence. A significant threat to human rights in one part of the world can and often has spread to other parts. If respect for the individual and individual rights were the cornerstone of a civil global society, then violations of these rights would have significant repercussions. When there is no concern for human rights, there is often no concern for democratic

FIGURE 4.1   The English Bill of Rights (1689)

Parliament, in 1689, drew up an act for securing the rights and liberties of English subjects. Known as the *English Bill of Rights,* this document limited the power of the King and listed the rights protected by Parliament.
    Among these were the following:

1. That the pretended power of suspending of laws, or the execution of laws, by regal authority, without the consent of Parliament, is illegal....
2. That levying money for or to the use of the crown....without grant of Parliament...is illegal.
5. That it is the right of the subjects to petition the king, and all commitments (arrests) and prosecutions for such petitioning is illegal.
6. That raising or keeping a standing army within the kingdom in time of peace, unless it be with consent of Parliament, is against law.
7. That the subjects which are Protestants may have arms for their defense as allowed by law.

Reprinted from Cotlin, J., & Palmer, R. (1995). *A history of the modern world.* New York: McGraw-Hill, p. 179.

FIGURE 4.2   **The French Declaration of the Rights of Man and Citizen (1789)**

Among the first reforms enacted during the French Revolution was a declaration by the National Assembly on August 27, 1789, that set forth the basic rights to which the Revolution was committed. This *Declaration of the Rights of Man and Citizen* embodied the hopes of people for a society based on liberty and equality. Among the natural rights of humankind that it recognized were the following:

- Men are born and remain free and equal in rights....
- The aim of every [government] is the preservation of the natural rights of man. These rights are liberty, property, security, and resistance to oppression.
- The law has the right to forbid only such actions as are injurious to society....
- Law is the expression of the general will. All citizens have the right to take part personally or by their representatives, in its formation. It must be the same for all, whether it protects or punishes....
- No man can be accused, arrested, or detained, except in cases determined by the law and according to the forms that it has prescribed....
- Every man [is] presumed innocent until he has been pronounced guilty...

Reprinted from Cotlin, J., & Palmer, R. (1995). *A history of the modern world.* New York: McGraw-Hill, p. 371.

governments, communities, or global environmental issues. The result is often chaos of major proportions.

What Are Human Rights?

Human rights are the fundamental values societies hold to be at the core of human dignity. They are an essential element of civilization. These rights ought to be promoted through education in order to have principled and active citizens who behave with moral and intellectual integrity. Practices that degrade human rights, such as sexism, racism, anti-Semitism, and discrimination, are antithetical to the principles of civil societies. It is incumbent upon the schools to promote a climate in which these practices are critically examined.

The United Nations Universal Declaration of Human Rights provides a positive blueprint that forces people to think about the current human condition and invites people to work on improving the human condition. The role of the teacher is to make students aware of the human rights accorded to all people by the United Nations Declaration and enable them to examine violations of these rights throughout the world.

Human rights education is important because it is a teaching approach based on the principles that all human beings are born equal and have the right to life, liberty, and the pursuit of happiness. These four principles are stated in both the preamble to the United States Constitution and in the United Nations Declaration of Human Rights. Each of these documents defines an ideal state of human rights and sets standards to be followed. The actual treatment of humans in much of today's world is nowhere near what is described in these two documents. One of the major goals of human rights education is to reduce the gap between the human rights that citizens of this world should be accorded and those rights they actually enjoy.

Why Should Teachers Be Concerned with Human Rights?

Teachers have a major role and responsibility in the promotion of good citizenship on the national and global levels. Such citizenship includes cultivating the capacity to make moral choices, holding principled positions on issues, and devising democratic courses of citizen action. If students were to demonstrate such behaviors, the major goals of human rights education would be accomplished. Teachers need to understand the issues underlying human rights—in particular, the importance of issues that undermine human dignity. Educators must be concerned with the human rights of people everywhere and present these issues to students for reflective analysis.

Women's Rights in the United States

The rights of women are a major concern in the world and should be of concern to all teachers. Questions of equal pay, jobs, educational opportunities, and equal standing in society are vital to the discussion of the rights of women in this society and the rest of the world. Teachers can clarify these issues and their concerns about them by using such questions as these: "Is it fair that girls who like to climb trees and play ball be called 'tomboys' because of what they like to do?" (at an early elementary level) and "Does the absence of an Equal Rights Amendment in the U.S. Constitution affect equality between men and women as citizens in our society?" (at a junior or senior high school level). These questions could be useful aids to promote good citizenship on the national level. Expanding the same issue (the rights of women) on a global level can be done with students at all ages by the use of facts revealing that in some societies, little girls are often not taught to read or write simply because they are girls.

One of the high points of the modern feminist movement was its success in getting the U.S. Congress to pass the proposed Equal Rights Amendment (ERA) which stated that "equality of rights under the law shall not be denied or abridged by the United States or by any State on account of sex." The amendment also provided the power to enforce it through appropriate legislation. This amendment was passed in Congress by an overwhelming margin in 1972 and was ratified by 30 state legislatures within a year. Supporters needed eight more states to ratify the ERA and had seven years to get them. Its approval seemed certain. Yet, 10 years later, even though Congress had extended the deadline, there were not enough ratifications to make the ERA the 27th amendment to the U.S. constitution. Some states that had ratified it wanted to rescind their ratifications. The ERA, which Betty Friedan once called, "the symbol and substance of the feminist movement," was ultimately defeated in 1982 (Macionis, 1997, p. 396). The defeat of the ERA left the United States without national constitutional protection against discrimination based on gender.

Much of the responsibility for the defeat of the ERA must go to the "Stop ERA" movement. This national organization focused on key states and persuaded state legislators to vote against ratification. Surprisingly, the movement was headed largely by women. Its leader, conservative activist Phyllis Schlafly, argued that the amendment would not help but would hurt women. Despite the seemingly simple language of the amendment, she predicted that crusading judges and bureaucrats would broaden it to promote abortion on demand, strike down alimony laws for women, and make them subject to the draft (Schlafly, 1977, p. 89).

Supporters of the ERA insisted that the legislative intent was simply to protect women's constitutional rights. Nothing feminists said reassured their opponents. Indeed, the opposition seemed to be directed as much at feminists as at the amendment. ERA opponents tended to be women from traditional backgrounds who regarded the new feminism as a threat. They resented what they saw as the feminists' contemptuous attitude toward housewives and worried aloud about the lesbian and "man-hating" factions in the movement. The opponents deplored the very style of modern-day feminism, which they considered coarse and unfeminine (Hunter, 1991, p. 42).

People in opposition to the ERA, who tended to focus on the female draft issue, did not address the lack of opportunity for women in the military (especially those who wished to make it their career) or the difficulty these women had in earning decision-making positions. The military women were sometimes denied access to such positions because they had no combat training or experience. Traditionally, women had served in clerical and nursing positions. However, since tax money supports the armed forces, should women be denied decision-making positions as well as the right to defend their country? A nonmilitary issue involving gender equity is whether women who make more money than their spouses (whom they are divorcing) should have to pay them alimony. The ERA could have had a bearing on these issues.

Most U.S. citizens today do not fall squarely into either the feminist or the anti-feminist camp. Most U.S. women seem to have ambivalent feelings about the movement that initiated the ERA. When respondents to a June 1989 *New York Times* poll were asked if the United States "continues to need a strong women's movement to push for changes that benefit women," 67% of the women responded, "Yes." When asked if women's organizations had done something to make their lives better, only 25% of the women agreed (Hunter, 1991, p. 42).

Women's Rights in Developing Nations

Female genital mutilation is another issue that has come into the spotlight, as young women from societies that maintain this practice are seeking political asylum in other countries. In 1980, the United Nations made a formal statement on its position regarding this topic.

To the United Nations Commission on Human Rights, it expressed unequivocal opposition to medicalization of the practice and strongly advised health workers not to perform female genital mutilation under any conditions. Moreover, the WHO has appealed for an end to the practice, which has been condemned by the organization's annual assembly for the last two years. In 1994, the World Health Assembly urged all member states "to establish national policies and programs that will effectively and with legal instruments, abolish female genital mutilation...and other harmful practices affecting the health of women and children" (Rourke, 1993, p. 557). In 1994, the Special Rapporteur on violence against women appointed by the Commission of Human Rights concluded that traditional practices, among which includes female genital mutilation, "should be constructed as a definite form of violence against women. This violence could not be overlooked nor be justified on the grounds of tradition, culture, or social conformity" (United Nations, 1994, p. 35).

It may appear that women in the United States have made phenomenal progress in the areas of equal pay, equal jobs, and equal opportunity. However, on a worldwide scale, significant progress is not evident. A 1991 United Nations study, *The World's Women 1970–1990,* reported alarming results (United Nations, 1991). In the workforce women were generally segregated from the men, placed in less prestigious and lower-paying jobs. In comparison to men, women's earnings ranged from half of what men earned (in countries such as Japan, South Korea, and Cyprus) to 71% of what males earned in Canada. Women were reported to have worked 13 hours more per week than men in Africa and Asia. Results of the study further reported that in 1985, the number of illiterate women had risen to 597 million compared to 352 million illiterate men (Cockerham, 1995, p. 219).

Why should teachers concern their students with the human rights of women? The facts below support the need for improvement in the circumstances of the world's women:

- Women perform two thirds of the world's work and earn only one tenth of the income.
- While growing 50% of the world's food, women only own 1% of its property.
- Two thirds of the world's illiterates are women.
- Nearly 1,500 women die every day because of complications from pregnancy and/or abortion (Kirdar, 1992, p. 13).

On a global level, the majority of women do not have equal standing with men in terms of power, wealth, and opportunity. Discrimination against them still persists on both a domestic and global front (Cockerham, 1995, p. 219).

In *Educating for Human Dignity: Learning About Rights and Responsibilities,* Reardon offers an array of suggestions for teaching human rights to students of all ages. She suggests that the teachers should do the following:

1. Comprehend that human dignity is only sustainable if we promote human rights, without which the world public order is at stake. Economic equity, equal opportunity, and the environment are all interconnected to the structure and process of life itself.
2. Be concerned with the application of human rights to the classroom in order to instill, through example, the human ethics and values for the world and its citizens.
3. Teach students the ability to transcend narrow self-interests and agree that the interest of the whole will be best served by accepting a set of common human values and rights.
4. Become the promoters of a broader global civil society, since without specific human values and ethics, the global society will become unfocused (Reardon, 1995, p. 5).

These suggestions by Reardon are important concepts for both human rights and global education.

Economic Relationships and Human Rights

Economics often affect the human rights of individuals. In most societies, there is a clear distinction between people who occupy different positions in the social class hierarchy. This hierarchy ranges from those people who "have" to those who "have not." How does this unequal distribution occur? Gerhard and Jean Lenski, using Darwin's theory of evolution as a model, developed a theory of sociocultural evolution that offers a suggestion to explain this unequal phenomenon. They proposed that social change follows technology rather than the other way around (Lenski, Nolan, & Lenski, 1996, p. 75.) and that four different types of societies evolved as a response to technological advancements. The four types of societies are the hunting–gathering, horticultural–pastoral, agrarian, and industrial (Macionis, 1997, pp. 97–101).

The Lenskis suggested that as humans were able to advance technologically and produce their own means of subsistence, a surplus emerged. People were able to produce more than they needed to consume. In time, this surplus generated wealth. Some individuals and groups produced and had more than others. In the agrarian society, which the Lenskis defined as "large scale agricultural production through the use of plows drawn by animals" (Cockerham, 1995, p. 134), the surplus produced created the emergence of a banking system (Cockerham, 1995, p. 134). As a result, this society produced a social stratification system that manifested greater inequality than its predecessors. Subsequently, the industrial societies that are prevalent in the world today have perpetuated this inequality in the distribution of wealth and the creation of social classes (Cockerham, 1995, p. 134).

Most societies today are characterized by an unequal distribution of wealth and a hierarchical social class system. This raises a variety of questions concerning human rights. How are human rights affected by this inequality? How is the right to life affected when food, medical care, and a safe and healthy environment are not readily available? How is the right to liberty affected when civil rights (e.g., freedom of speech), political rights (e.g., the right to vote), and social rights (e.g., the right to protection from economic insecurity, i.e., welfare system) are absent? How is the pursuit of happiness possible when one is starving or being persecuted? (Cockerham, 1995, p. 367)

Economics have an effect on human rights. Over half of the world's population lives in poverty (Rourke, 548–563). Many countries are governed by military or political dictatorships, and fifteen million refugees are seeking the right to life, liberty and the pursuit of happiness (UNHCR: The State of the World's Refugees, 50). Presenting these issues to students is a way for them to understand the dynamics of how economics affect the rights of individuals.

In addition to discussing these issues, a teacher can pose a variety of questions. For example, "How did the United States and the rest of the world respond to the Iraqi invasion of Kuwait, the murder of the Chinese students at Tiananmen Square, or the massive human exodus from Cuba since 1959?" Each of these events has affected human rights. How have military responses, political and economic sanctions, and economic embargoes helped people and their human rights in countries where these activities have occurred. What are the short term and long term impacts of such actions?" Discussions prompted by these questions can allow students to develop a critical approach to problem solving, as well as a sense of empathy and global responsibility.

The Teacher's Role in Human Rights Education

The teacher has to be proactive when presenting human rights issues in the classroom. The teaching of human rights needs to be woven into the core curriculum of schools in the United States. Teachers must be the catalysts if this goal is to be reached. Students and teachers can probe the idea that human rights involve the underlying concerns of a global ethic of human dignity. Teachers can introduce the concept of an ideal global civic society. This ideal society is defined as one in which "all citizens, as individuals and as members of different private groups and associations, should accept the obligation to recognize and help protect the rights of others" (The Commission on Global Governance, 1995, p. 56).

Respect for the individual is a key aspect of human rights. Elementary teachers illustrate this concept to students when they introduce the ideals of the American Revolution. Respect for the individual is further reinforced when students are taught about the writing of the United States Constitution and its Bill of Rights. The curriculum needs to establish a stronger link between the individual rights enjoyed by citizens of the United States and the individual rights accorded or not accorded to most of the world's population. Without an awareness of the uniqueness of each individual and a respect for human rights, there can be little basis for the expansion of democracy or a stable foundation for peace in the world.

POPULATION

Population is a seminal issue for global education and one that is easily brought into the curriculum at all grade levels. A social studies or geography class can provide an opportunity to focus on population and bring about global awareness and interdependence. In the early elementary grades, discussion of population could include comparisons of landmasses to the number of persons and resources available for each land area.

In the middle school years, a comparison of the state of Montana to the southeast Asian country of Bangladesh could be used. Montana has fewer than one million people, while Bangladesh, with about the same land area, has a population of 120 million. Bangladesh also has fewer resources per person than Montana. Based upon its current growth rate, Bangladesh is expected to double its population to 240 million in the next 30 years. What does this mean? Why or how does this happen? What can be done? These questions could provide a critical thinking exercise in the global education classroom. It is important for students to understand the demographic realities of the world's population. Students need to be made aware of the varying rates of population growth throughout the world and analyze the implications.

Theory, Patterns, and Factors of Population

In order to clearly understand the issue of population, one must take into consideration global population patterns and how modernization affects population growth. U.S. demographer, Frank Notestein (1969), suggests in his demographic transition theory that global population growth has occurred in three basic stages:

1. *The Pre-Modern Stage:* A high birth rate complemented by a high death rate creates a slow rate of population growth.
2. *The Early Industrial Stage:* A high birth rate complemented by a low death rate (attributed to the introduction of medical technologies) creates a fast rate of population growth.
3. *The Mature Industrial Stage:* Birthrates drop approximately to the point of being equal to a low death rate, which creates a slow population growth. (Ross, 1982, pp. 396–397, 536–543).

There are three basic factors that contribute to population change on a global scale. Technological advances in medicine have allowed for a longer life span and a lower infant mortality rate. The second factor is the forced migration of populations fleeing adverse governmental policies or seeking economic betterment. A third significant factor contributing to increases in population is cultural and religious practice in many of the developing countries, for which the number of children in a family is a sign of male virility. In some cases, families need a large number of children to look after parents in their old age or to work on family-owned farms. Using Notestein's theory as a framework along with these basic factors, one can understand why Montana's population is less than Bangladesh's.

A demographic study of the world today shows that of its 6 billion plus inhabitants, some 4.5 billion live in some of the poorest countries and suffer terrible conditions (Rourke, 1993, p. 548–563). Nearly 100 million people, roughly the equivalent to the population of Mexico, are added to the world each year. More than 90% of this population increase is added to the developing world (Cockerham, 1995, p. 235). According to *The World Health Report 1996*, 140 million babies were born in 1995 (World Health Organization, 1997). Of these, 16 million were born in the industrialized world, 25 million in the least developed countries, and 98 million in other developing countries (World Health Organization, 1997, p. 3). This rapid population growth produces adverse effects on developing nations' social and economic progress in a variety of ways.

Population growth consumes a great portion of resources that the country might otherwise use for investment in development. For example, if greater funding is needed in social services such as health and education, higher worker output is required to support these services. Therefore, greater pressure on limited agricultural land and/or natural resources is exerted (Mumford, 1966, p. 471). In essence, rapid population growth acts as an agent of poverty for developing nations. Limited resources, coupled with rapid population growth and the problems it creates, have hindered the development of many countries. This leaves many citizens of the world living in dire poverty.

The United Nations forecasts that by the year 2025, the world's population will be 10 billion people (Cockerham, 1995, p. 235). Nations need to concern themselves with what resources are available to maintain such a population and the subsequent growth a world population of 10 billion could produce. Awareness is also needed of the environmental consequences that result from the population of the earth growing by nearly 100 million people per year. Population pressures have significant adverse effects on the planet's ecology. Among these are the following:

- a loss of topsoil
- desertification of formerly productive farmland
- continuous burning of fossil fuels leading to a depletion of the ozone layer
- depleted ozone contributing to a gradual warming of the earth.

Teachers should explore with their students the relationship between natural resources and population. While technology is increasing the agricultural capacity of the world, most of the nearly 100 million new inhabitants of the planet are born to developing nations with limited access to the benefits of improved agricultural technology. A careful analysis of the relationship between the world's population and natural resources is a necessary component of the school's curriculum. Without this knowledge, students will be perplexed by many of the issues and tensions in today's and tomorrow's world.

Managing Population Growth

What can be done to manage global population growth? Can or should the world's nations attempt this task? Teachers should explore population management with students and prepare them for the challenges that lay ahead. In September 1994, the United Nations International Conference on Population and Development (ICPD) was held in Cairo, Egypt. Representatives from 179 nations endorsed a 20 year Plan for Action to stabilize the planet's population. This plan addressed the fertility of the earth, farm technology, fertilizers, pesticides, irrigation, and the ability of humankind to feed itself. Highlighted at the conference was the prospect of continued demographic growth, which raised disturbing questions. These questions did not merely address food supplies, but also addressed the capacity of the earth to withstand the impact of increased human consumption due to increases in population. In brief, the Plan for Action proposed education as the best channel for population management.

The success or failure of this plan could well mean the difference between the earth's population leveling off at 7–9 billion or its reaching 10–14 billion. It is only through education and training in developing countries that significant population management can be accomplished. This education on population issues will be a long-term and sometimes difficult process. If it is to succeed, family planning education must take into consideration people's local cultures and beliefs.

Women and Family Planning

The empowerment of many of the world's women and the improvement of their health, political, social, and economic status is an important issue of human rights as well as of population management. Five hundred million women worldwide need family planning but lack either the information or the means to obtain services. Education is one of the most important means of providing women with the knowledge, skills, and self-confidence to participate fully in the development process. High birth rates are often the result of inadequate information about birth control, as well as its availability. Other contributing factors to higher birth rates are high infant and child mortality rates and parents' need for support in old age (Mumford, 1996, p. 68).

There is no question that education plays a vital part in meeting the population challenge the world is experiencing. More than 40 years ago, the United Nations Declaration of Human Rights asserted that "everyone has the right to education" (Laqueur & Rubin, 1989, p. 201). In 1990, governments meeting in Thailand at the World Conference on Education for All committed themselves to the goal of universal access to basic education (United Nations, 1994, Report A/Conf. 171/13, p. 25). An important facet of education is reaching the adults. Women's ability to know about contraception as well as having pre- and postnatal health care is of paramount importance. This education of women is one of the few ways to improve the health of mothers and infants and to ensure voluntary reduction in population numbers. In 1995, an international gathering of women in Nairobi, Kenya, assessed women's progress during the 1980s and 1990s. According to the Nairobi conference, "All couples and individuals have the basic human right to decide freely and informally the number and spacing of their children; maternal and child health care should be strengthened; and family planning information should be widespread" (United Nations Department of Public Information, 1986, p. 39).

A more direct measure of population control is pursued in China, which constitutes approximately one fifth of the world's population. In 1978, the government of China initiated a birth control policy of one child per family (Cockerham, 1995, p. 228). Greenhalgh states,

> Enforcing such drastic changes in the marriage and childbearing habits of a billion people was no easy matter. Implementation was to rely on education in the benefits of small families, coupled with economic and administrative incentives for compliance with reproductive rules and, after 1979, penalties for having [additional] births. (Greenhalgh, 1990, p. 74)

The program was successful. The fertility rate dropped from 5.8 births per woman in 1970 to 2.8 per woman in 1987 (Cockerham, 1995, p. 228).

High school teachers could have a discussion comparing the Chinese method of population management with the Nairobi conference's proposal to give couples freedom to choose the number of children to have. This would produce an atmosphere in which students could raise a number of questions. Is it fair to limit the number of children a couple can have? Who decides how many children can be born? Are there other ways to control population growth?

The issue of population can provide important information for students of all ages to consider. An important caveat, however, is that information and questions about population issues should be presented to students in an age-appropriate manner. Charts and graphs can be used to illustrate current information and future forecasts and to provide a source for discussion. Students of all ages need to understand that population is one of the factors determining the demands on the world's resources.

REFUGEES

> Give me your tired, your poor, your huddled masses yearning to breathe free, The wretched refuse of your teeming shore. Send these, the homeless, tempest-tost to me, I lift my lamp beside the Golden Door. Emma Lazarus (Sima, 1993, p. 52)

In the world today there are some 15 million refugees (United Nations High Commissioner for Refugees, 1995, p. 20). Figure 4.3

FIGURE 4.3   The State of the World's Refugees

The world's major refugee situations: UNHCR is providing protection and assistance to 27.4 million people around the world, of whom 14.5 million are refugees.

War in former Yugoslavia
Some 3.7 million people who have been displaced or affected by the war are receiving humanitarian assistance from the United Nations, 2.7 million of them in Bosnia and Herzegovina alone.

Asylum in Europe
Since the early 1980s, around five million applications for refugee status have been submitted in Western Europe. UNHCR tries to ensure that any measures taken to control this phenomenon are consistent with the principles of refugee protection.

The Palestinian question
Around 2.8 million people are registered with UNRWA, the agency responsible for Palestinian refugees. Their future remains one of the most complex issues which must be addressed in the Middle East peace process.

West African refugees
The conflicts in Liberia and Sierra Leone have forced almost a million people into exile in Guinea and Cote d'Ivoire. Large numbers are also displaced within their own countries, beyond the reach of international assistance.

Guatemalan repatriation
Some 20,000 Guatemalans have returned to their homeland over the past 10 years. Up to a quarter of the 45,000 who remain in Mexico are expected to repatriate in 1995 with assistance from UNHCR.

Haitian asylum seekers
UNHCR is assisting with procedures designed to determine the status of asylum seekers from Haiti and to monitor the situation of those who return.

Reintegration in Mozambique
More than 1.6 million refugees returned to Mozambique from six neighbouring states between late 1992 and early 1995. They must now begin to support themselves and to reintegrate within their own communities.

From United Nations High Commissioner for Refugees (1995).
The state of the world's refugees: In search of solutions. New York: Oxford.

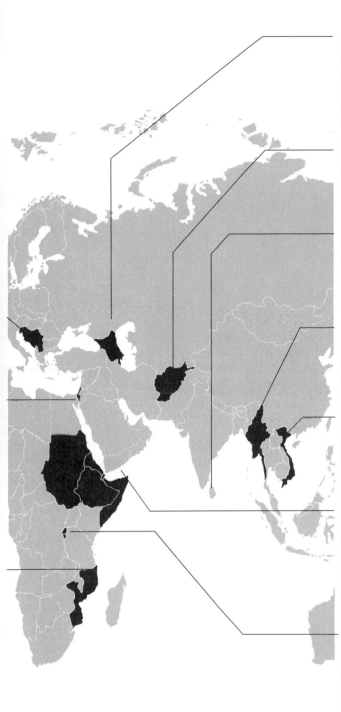

Conflicts in Caucasus
Recent years have witnessed a succession of population displacements within and between Armenia, Azerbaijan, Georgia and the Russian Federation, involving around 1.5 million people. Many of this number are unable or unwilling to return to their former place of residence.

Reconstruction in Afghanistan
Half of the Afghan refugees have repatriated since 1992, leaving nearly three million in the Islamic Republic of Iran and Pakistan. Additional reconstruction efforts are needed within Afghanistan to enable their return.

Displaced Sri Lankans
More than 30,000 Sri Lankan refugees have returned from India since 1992, leaving nearly 75,000 in their country of asylum. UNHCR provides assistance to the returnees and to other people who are threatened or displaced by the war.

Repatriation to Myanmar
By mid-1995, only 50,000 of the 250,000 people who fled from Myanmar in 1991 and 1992 remained in Bangladesh. The homeward movement, organized by UNHCR, is scheduled for completion by the end of the year.

Vietnamese boat people
Although the departure of boat people has effectively come to a halt, just over 40,000 Vietnamese asylum seekers remain in camps throughout South-East Asia. More than 70,000 have gone back to their own country, where their situation is monitored by UNHCR.

The Horn of Africa: exile and repatriation
UNHCR continues to assist around 1.6 million people from the Horn of Africa and the Sudan, traditionally one of the most important refugee-producing regions. The repatriation to Eritrea from Sudan is finally under way, more than 30 years after the first refugees left that country.

The Rwanda/Burundi emergency
More than a million Rwandese poured into Zaire in mid-1994, one of the largest and fastest refugee movements ever seen. UNHCR is now providing protection and assistance to some 2.2 million displaced people in Burundi, Rwanda, Tanzania, Uganda and Zaire.

provides an illustration of the areas that have created the refugees of today's world. One of the greatest challenges of the twenty-first century is to ensure that people in every part of the world can enjoy security and freedom. People who do not live with security, freedom, and a means of subsistence are often left with no alternative but to flee from their homeland and seek refuge in another country. These forced migrations may in turn generate new forms of tension and insecurity. According to the United Nations High Commissioner for Refugees (UNHCR), as a result of the most recent succession of refugee emergencies, refugees are increasingly confronted with rejection and exclusion, (UNHCR, 1995, p. 8).

The use of refugee issues is most appropriate in U.S. classrooms as a tool to promote global education. Teachers may use examples of refugees in U.S. history to introduce the topic. From early elementary to secondary education, all students can appreciate the plight of people in search of refuge. The Pilgrims could serve as a good example of this concept. Why did the Pilgrims come? What were they looking for? How did they survive and adjust when they came? How are the people arriving on boats and rafts from Caribbean nations different from or similar to the Pilgrims? Answers to these questions help students understand individuals' quest for freedom from persecution and hunger. In order to strengthen national and global citizenship, students must comprehend the problems that create refugees in the world today. Why is the refugee issue so important? As Figure 4.4 clearly illustrates, the United States hosts the largest concentration of refugees in the world. Refugees are not only fellow citizens of the world, but they are part of U.S. communities, neighborhoods, classrooms, and personal relationships.

A refugee can be defined as someone who is forced to migrate. Reasons for forced migrations are political and religious persecution and the lack of national governmental protection. The inability to meet basic economic needs in one's homeland also creates many refugees. The reasons that create refugee populations are complex. Persons may be individually persecuted, they may be fleeing a war, or they may be unable to take care of their families in their country of origin. Any one or combination of these reasons can cause people to leave their nations and become refugees. The remainder of the chapter focuses on some of these dynamics that cause human displacement.

Political Causes

The 1951 Convention and the 1967 Protocol on the Status of Refugees identified what is still a major problem for refugees: persecution based on race, nationality, religion, or ethnicity (UNHCR, 1994). Persecution can occur as a consequence of a number of political questions. Who will be in charge of the state? Who has power? Who controls the economy, patronage, and benefits? In many instances, this struggle for and the maintenance of power brings about an oppression of opposition. These disputes intensify during violent changes of government, revolutionary wars, civil wars, and the emergence of new nations. Entire social classes and ethnic groups may be annihilated because they hold economic and political power or hold political opinions in opposition to the state. For example, many professionals in Cambodia were killed under the Pol Pot government. The Kurds in Turkey, Iran, and Iraq have also been the victims of significant persecution. The vast majority of refugees flee because they are either targeted for persecution or suffer from generalized violence. This violence is often from the armed opposition of the state organizations, such as the Tupac Amaru in Peru, the Rnamo in Mozambique, the Khmer Rouge in Cambodia, and the Bosnian Serbs. Violence destroys the fabric of civil society. When persons do not side with the government or the rebel group, they can become the targets of violence. Individual safety cannot be guaranteed and a refugee exodus soon follows.

Economic Causes

Another major cause of refugees is economic tension. Deterioration of economic standing among individuals or groups frequently stems from efforts to preserve the standing of one individual or group at the expense of another. Disputes concerning the distribution of resources during periods of economic decline are often politically explosive. One has only to look at Russia's present economic problems and the growing number of persons wanting to return to a communist system. During difficult economic times, minority groups are often turned into scapegoats. Adolf Hitler blamed most of the economic difficulties experienced by Germans during the Great Depression on Europe's Jews.

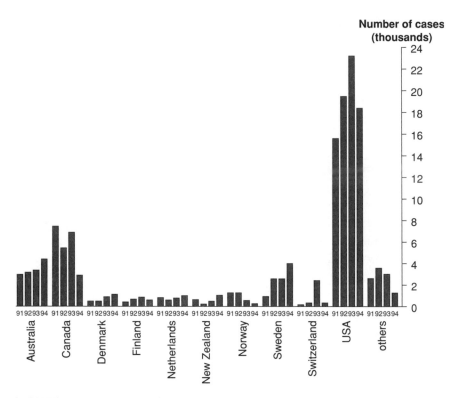

FIGURE 4.4   UNHCR Resettlement Cases by Receiving Country, 1991–1994

From United Nations High Commissioner for Refugees (1995). *The State of the World's Refugees, 1995: In search of solutions*. Washington, DC: Author. Reprinted by permission of the United Nations High Commissioner for Refugees.

Poverty often exacerbates ethnic and communal tensions. During the 1950s and 1960s, it was believed that development in the world's poorer countries would be a speedy and irreversible process, due in part to the high level of demand for their export products (UNHCR, 1995, p. 144). This was not the case. Population growth and a lack of natural resources are conducive to poverty, not development, regardless of product demand. When nearly all of a society's resources are needed to keep up with rising population, they are not available for development. For example, "The gap between needs and available resources in Africa is widening...per capita incomes have continued falling in the 1990s and marked deterioration has taken place in essential social services, especially education and health care" (UNHCR, 1995, p. 154). In Ghana, the per capita income is $390 annually, and worse is Chad's annual per capita income of $133 (Cockerham, 1995, p. 196).

More than one billion people worldwide live in poverty (UNHCR, 1995, p. 15). In many near-subsistence economies, violent conflict disrupts food production and distribution and displaces people. In Sudan's civil war, many Sudanese have starved or succumbed to diseases that they would probably have been able to resist had the political situation been more stable. Violent conflict undoubtedly contributes to economic stagnation and human displacement.

Environmental Causes

Millions of human beings have been forced to leave their homes because the land on which they had lived became uninhabitable and was no longer able to support them. In some cases, such as the eruption of Mount Pinatubo in the Philippines, the cause is a natural disaster. In other cases, the cause is manmade. Examples of the latter are the spread of radiation due to the meltdown of the Chernobyl reactor in the former Soviet Union or the spread of a desert due to deforestation. In extreme cases, the destruction of habitat is a deliberate weapon of war. The use of the defoliant Agent Orange in Vietnam is an example of this. There are links between environmental degradation and the flow of refugees. The deterioration of the natural resource base, coupled with demographic pressure and poverty, lead to conflicts that force people to flee. Haiti and Somalia are nations where this has occurred.

Ethnic Tensions

Conflicts caused by ethnic differences and hatred have been rampant in recent years. The genocide (see Figure 4.5) in Bosnia-Herzegovina is an example of the extreme actions caused by ethnic hatred. Somalia, Rwanda, Burundi, Chechnya, and Iraq are nations where people have been killed solely because of their ethnic backgrounds. Very few nations of the world are ethnically homogeneous today. Among the 190 member countries of the United Nations, there are approximately 5,000 ethnic groups. Ethnic diversity is part of human geography almost everywhere on the planet.

FIGURE 4.5   Genocide

Genocide is the denial to groups of the right to live. It is the deliberate destruction of racial, ethnic, national or religious groups. Although the commitment of genocide has inflicted great suffering on humanity throughout history, there was no clear awareness of it as a general crime until the twentieth century.

It was more precisely defined in 1948 when the General Assembly of the United Nations adopted *The Convention on the Prevention and Punishment of the Crime of Genocide*. This document clarifies genocide in terms of the killing or the causing of bodily or mental harm with the intent to destroy, in whole or in part, a national, ethnic, racial or religious group.

Reprinted from Forsythe, D. (1989). *Human rights and world politics*. Lincoln, NE: University of Nebraska Press, p. 11.

How do these "ethnic cleansings" come about? Despite the fact that most countries contain a variety of ethnic groups, the identity of a single large ethnic group is frequently made the defining characteristic of the national identity. Generally, this national ethnic identity carries with it power, opportunity, and greater social status over the other ethnic groups. This condition provides a tension for potential conflict, unless assimilation into the dominant ethnic identity occurs or influence is shared democratically among groups. Today, the notion of an ethnically pure nation–state is largely a fantasy that can only be realized at an unacceptably high human cost (UNCHR, 1995, p. 20).

It is important for students to understand that turmoil and internal strife in a nation affect all parts of the society. Even the lives of those in control are disrupted when nations do not enjoy stability. In spite of the difficulties in the United States, these problems do not compare with those faced by many citizens of the developing world. U.S. students understand the turmoil caused by natural disasters such as hurricanes, earthquakes, and other weather-induced catastrophes. Using these as examples, a teacher could point out that people affected by natural disasters can begin to clean up and start anew when the storm passes.

By comparison, the plight of the refugee seems to be unending. The misery refugees experience in their home countries does not last a few hours or even a few days. It is often indefinite. The choices afforded to individuals in these situations are few. Why would members of a Haitian family risk their lives by traveling with little or no food on a small boat in hopes of reaching the United States? What is the likelihood that Haitian refugees will find a haven or be deported? How is their experience similar or different from someone who is a victim of a flood? What are the choices and opportunities that each has in building a new life or starting over? Encouraging students to relate to the experiences of refugees will help them develop empathy and understanding.

Educators can use the issue of refugees to teach global citizenship and responsibility. It is an effective topic that lends itself to presenting concepts such as prejudice, discrimination, persecution, and displacement. Older students can explore the beliefs of "hate groups," such as the Nazis and the Ku Klux Klan, that support ethnic cleansing in the United States. These groups' opinions can be compared to the attitudes of groups such as the Serbs in Bosnia toward Muslim Bosnians. Teachers can invite survivors of the Holocaust to visit and speak with students so that the students can hear, firsthand, the horror of persecution. It is likely that refugees are available in the school's community to visit and share their experiences. Talking about real people's lives is a way to reach students and emphasize the responsibility all people share in solving the world's problems.

It will be the challenge of today's students, as leaders in the twenty-first century, to alleviate economic, political, environmental, and ethnic tensions and to create a more stable and civil global society. Their success, and the stability of the world, depends significantly on how the issues presented in this chapter are addressed. The tension between technological and moral development is captured by Dr. Martin Luther King, Jr. as follows:

> Through our scientific genius, we have made of the world a neighborhood; but now through moral and spiritual genius we must make of it a brotherhood. (Provensen, 1995, p. 54)

SUMMARY

As human societies evolved, an interdependent relationship developed between people. Beginning as independent food producers, humans slowly created new items such as clothing, housing, furniture, and utensils that became a necessary part of their lives. In time, the weaver made clothes, the farmer grew food, and each was dependent on the other to fulfill a particular need. Today, students can witness the interdependence between their country and the rest of the world through the products available to them. Global education's purpose is not only to introduce and illustrate interdependence to students, but to generate a sense of global responsibility in them. A variety of issues can be discussed by the teacher to begin the recognition of and responsibility for global concerns. These issues could be social change, population issues, natural and human resources, development and education issues, violence and peace issues, and human rights issues.

Human rights should be an integral part of the core curriculum. Teaching respect for human rights helps to contribute to an equitable and more civil global society. Students need to be made aware of the human rights accorded to them in the preamble to the United States Constitution and the United Nations Declaration of Human Rights. These rights of life, liberty, and the pursuit of happiness, as well as the principle that all human beings are born equal, are fundamental. Students need to be aware of the gap between the rights that world citizens should be accorded and those they actually enjoy.

An examination of the rights of women across the globe can specifically illustrate the gap between accorded rights and those actually enjoyed. Questions of equal pay, jobs, educational opportunity, and standing in society can be used for examination. A look into the history of the Equal Rights Amendment in the United States can show students that there were and are differences between the rights granted to men and women and that a social movement emerged to address them. Issues such as genital mutilation, illiteracy rates, lack of prenatal health care, and the imbalance of income can clarify problems still facing many of the world's women. Teachers should remember that potentially controversial content should be presented to students in an age-appropriate manner.

Students should understand the unequal distribution of wealth at the national and international levels. What happens to human rights in severe economic conditions? Can an individual pursue the rights to life, liberty, and the pursuit of happiness when their basic needs are not met? When students discover that over half the world's population lives in poverty, the issue of human rights takes on a new dimension. An examination of repressive government actions against its citizens, such as the murder of Chinese students in Tiananmen Square, can provide students in the global classroom with the chance to think about the right to liberty.

Teachers should be proactive when presenting such issues in the classroom. Human rights need to be incorporated into the core curriculum in U.S. schools. The curriculum should establish a link between the rights enjoyed by U.S. citizens and the rights accorded to people in the rest of the world. This can serve as a basis for the expansion of democracy and world peace.

A focus on population can bring about greater global awareness. Students can explore population growth across the globe through the study of three basic factors. Medical technology, migration, and cultural and religious practices affect population increases. Where do population increases occur at greater rates in the world? Of the 140 million babies born in 1995, 98 million were born in developing nations. This increase in population creates concern regarding what resources are available to accommodate the needs of the earth's inhabitants. Nearly 4.5 billion of the 6 billion people of the world today live in poverty. How can the world respond? Are attempts to curtail the growth of the world's population an appropriate answer?

In 1994, the United Nations International Conference on Population and Development endorsed a 20 year plan to stabilize the earth's population. The plan proposed education and family planning as a channel for population management. High birth rates are often the result of inadequate access to birth control. Education in family planning would provide the world's women the knowledge, skills, and self-confidence to control their fertility and make decisions about the size of their families. There are over 500 million women worldwide who would greatly benefit from family planning education and the ability to obtain birth control. Older students could explore policies such as China's one child per family. They could question the impact such a law could have on human rights as well as population growth.

A look at the 15 million refugees in the world today illustrates that not all people in the world enjoy security, freedom, or means of subsistence. Students can look at their own communities and their televisions to discover that the United States hosts the largest concentration of refugees of any nation in the world. There are a variety of causes that force individuals to migrate. People migrate for political reasons, such as those caused by a repressive government's persecution. Economics is another cause; individuals leave their homes in pursuit of better economic conditions and survival. Environmental problems, such as those caused by natural disasters, force people to relocate. Persecution based on religious or ethnic differences is also a great incentive for migration. Students in the United States should become aware of the turmoil that affects daily life in other parts of the world. Specific case studies can provide the awareness. If refugees from the community visit the students, the classroom can also be very effective.

Students will be challenged with these issues as leaders in the twenty-first century. They need to understand economic, environmental, and political tensions in today's and tomorrow's world. Their ability to understand the world in which they live depends on how global issues are addressed in the classroom.

SUGGESTED ACTIVITIES

Elementary

Objectives

- To learn about refugee conditions in the world.
- To know about the plight of refugees.
- To appreciate how refugees start a new life.

Activity

Present background information and the personal stories of refugees. Point out that women and children make up 75% of the world's refugees. On a large map of the world in the classroom, point out or mark from where the refugees you discuss emigrated. Invite a recent refugee in your community to come and speak to the class. Ask the speaker to point out the speaker's home country on the map and speak about the experience of leaving home and starting a new life. Students should ask questions such as, What was it like in your home country? Did you make friends when you came here? Were people nice to you when you came? How many things could you bring with you from your country? Why did you leave your country? Do you like it here? Were you scared leaving your country and coming here? How did you come to the United States?

Follow-up
Have each student write a note to the speaker and the speaker's family thanking them for sharing their story. Discuss the speaker's visit and reinforce the information provided. Ask students to write what they learned about refugees and how refugees start a new life.

Middle School

Objectives

- To comprehend the magnitude of population growth.
- To explore where the greatest concentration of population growth is occurring.
- To know and identify the following terms: fertility rate, mortality rate, and infant mortality rate resources.
- To comprehend the importance of stabilizing population growth.

Activity
Have students research population statistics for nations around the world. (Be sure that fertility rates, infant mortality rates, and poverty levels are included.) Also, instruct students to research population growth projections. Have the class mark a world map to note where the heaviest concentrations of people are in the world. Then ask the class to create a cause and effect chart that shows the many social and environmental consequences linked to unabated population growth.

Follow-up
Quiz the students on population terms. Ask them to brainstorm ways to manage population growth or ways to enhance resource production and use.

High School

Objectives

- To evaluate the human rights dimensions of issues.
- To comprehend the events involved in the Tiananmen Square incident in China.

- To compare and contrast the human rights accorded to students in the United States to those accorded to the students in China.

Activity

Have the students research the uprising of college students in the Tiananmen Square incident that occurred in China in 1989. They should create a chart of the issues the Chinese students addressed. Have them compare the issues to their own lives. Ask them to debate whether the Chinese government's response to the students was acceptable. Ask them to identify the cultural issues or special conditions the Chinese students had to consider before deciding to stage their protest in Tiananmen Square.

Follow-up

Have students write an essay using the Tiananmen Square incident as an example. Ask them to explain why there are or are not certain rights that should be universal.

QUESTIONS FOR REFLECTION

1. Should human rights be universal? If not, what objections do you have? What clarifications or conditions might you attach?
2. There are nations where human rights have been denied or violated. Choose an example and examine it. What rights were denied? How did the elimination of rights affect individuals and the society? How did the world respond? How was the situation resolved (if applicable)?
3. Examine human rights in the United States. Have they historically been accorded to all citizens and residents? Do all U.S. citizens currently enjoy them? If not, who are the individuals or groups that are lacking these rights? Have conditions improved? What social movements have emerged to address them?
4. What explanations can you offer to account for the inequality of income when men and women perform similar work?
5. Should actions be taken to ensure that human rights are available to all people across the globe? If so, what would you recommend?
6. What are the social and environmental consequences of rapid population growth in developing countries? What are some of the causes? Can

it be stabilized? What have some nations done to address the issue? How has the world responded?

7. What are some causes that have forced people to leave their homes and become refugees?

8. What are the key problems that people face when they become refugees? How are they solved?

REFERENCES

Bartlett, J. (1980). *Familiar quotations.* Boston: Little, Brown, & Company.

Cockerham, W. (1995). *The global society: An introduction to sociology.* New York: McGraw-Hill.

The Commission on Global Governance. (1995). *Our global neighborhood.* (Report of the Commission on Global Governance). Oxford, England: Oxford University Press.

Cotlin, J., & Palmer, R. (1995). *A history of the modern world.* New York: McGraw-Hill.

Forsythe, D. (1989). *Human rights and world politics.* Lincoln, NE: University of Nebraska Press.

Greenhalgh, S. (1990). Socialism and fertility in China. *Annals of the American Academy of Political and Social Science, 510,* 73–86.

Hunter, J. (1991). *Culture wars: The struggle to define America.* New York: Basic Books.

Kirdar, U. (1992). *Change: Threat or opportunity? Social change.* New York: United Nations.

Laqueur, W., & Rubin, B. (1989). *The human rights reader.* Markham, Ontario: Penguin.

Lenski, G., Nolan, P., & Lenski, J. (1996). *Human societies: An introduction to macrosociology* (7th ed.). New York: McGraw-Hill.

Macionis, J. J. (1997). *Sociology* (6th ed.). Englewood Cliffs, NJ: Prentice-Hall.

Mumford, S. (1966). *The life and death of NSSM 200: How the destruction of political will doomed a U.S. population policy.* Research Triangle Park, NC: Center for Research of Population and Security.

Notestein, F. W. (1969). *Economic problems of population change.* Indianapolis, IN: Bobbs-Merrill College Division.

Provensen, A. (1995). *My fellow Americans.* New York: Harcourt Brace.

Reardon, B. (1995). *Educating for human dignity: Learning about rights and responsibilities.* Philadelphia: University of Pennsylvania.

Ross, J. A. (1982). *International encyclopedia of population* (Vol. 2.). New York: The Free Press.

Rourke, J. (1993). *International politics on the world stage.* Guilford, CT: Dushkin-McGraw-Hill.

Schlafly, P. (1977). *The power of the positive woman* (6th ed.). New Rochelle, NY: Arlington House.

Sima, P. (1993). *Thematic unit: Immigration.*Huntington Beach, CA: Teacher Created Materials.

United Nations. (1980). World Conference of the United Nations Decade for Women: Equality, Development, and Peace, Copenhagen, Denmark.

United Nations. (1991). *The world's women, 1970–1990: Trends and statistics.* New York: United Nations.

United Nations. (1994, February 23). *The declaration of the elimination of violence against women.* Forty-Eighth Session of the General Assembly of the UN, Agenda Item 111, A/RES/48/104.

United Nations. (1994, September 5–13). United Nations International Conference on Population and Development, Cairo, Egypt. (Report A/Conf. 171/13)

United Nations. (1994, October 18). *Report of the United Nations International Conference on Population and Development.* (Report A/Conf. 171/13)

United Nations Department of Public Information: Division for Economic and Social Information. (1986, December). *The 1995 Nairobi forward-looking strategies for the advancement of women.* New York: United Nations.

United Nations General Assembly. (1948, December 10). *Universal declaration of human rights.* Minneapolis, MN: Human Rights USA Resource Center.

United Nations High Commissioner for Refugees. (1994). *Children: Guidelines on protection and care.* Geneva, Switzerland: Author.

United Nations High Commissioner for Refugees. (1995). *The state of the world's refugees: In search of solutions.* New York: Oxford University.

World Health Organization. (1997, February 3). Executive summary. *The World Health 1996.* Available: www.who.ch/whr/1996/exsume.htm

5

GLOBAL ISSUES: ENVIRONMENT, ENERGY, HEALTH, AND NUTRITION

Major Points

- The biosphere is composed of the atmosphere, soil, water, and living organisms.

- The burning of fossil fuels has influenced a gradual warming of the earth's climate.

- Soil erosion and deforestation have had very adverse effects on the world's environment.

- Nuclear energy has distinct advantages and disadvantages.

- Malnutrition and vitamin and mineral deficiencies create major health problems in much of the world.

- International organizations have attempted to alleviate environmental problems with limited success.

We are living in a time of rapid change in an increasingly complex world. There is little doubt that humanity's survival depends on its increased respect for the environment. Human beings are closely related to and dependent on all the life on earth. Concern over destruction of the environment, perhaps more than any

The authors wish to acknowledge the assistance of Victoria Samaras Polentas with the preparation of this chapter.

other issue, has helped crystallize the notion that all members of humanity share a common destiny. The dilemma is how to reconcile economic activity and rising population with maintaining a healthy environment.

Approaching environmental issues from a bio-centric (earth-centered) perspective and contrasting this with an anthropocentric (human-centered) approach is an effective way for teachers to present environmental issues. A bio-centric approach supports the concept of harmonious evolution of humanity and the bioenvironment and it suggests that economic activity influencing the bioenvironment should be conducted without creating adverse environmental effects. Teachers could raise the following questions concerning the environment with the students: What is the place of human beings in the natural world? Do humans have a responsibility to other species? Is human destiny entwined with the destiny of other life forms? Do human beings destroy or develop the natural world, or do they accept the natural world as it is and conform to it? The following facts suggest the delicate nature of the bioenvironment:

- 200 elephants are killed every day.
- 25,000 to 50,000 square kilometers of Brazilian rainforests are destroyed every year.
- Exotic animals are trapped for sale in different parts of the world.
- Desertification has caused the loss of 9% of the arable land in the world during the 1980s and 1990s.
- Dioxin, an extremely toxic compound, has accumulated in the fish of the Baltic Sea to such an extent that it has been detected in the blood plasma of fish-eating people (Harms, 1994, pp. 233–248; *Environmental Encyclopedia,* 1994, pp. 80–82, 321–322).

This information can lead to discussions with students about the health and economic issues involved in environmental studies. Why are so many elephants killed each day? Why are the rainforests being chopped down? What effect does dioxin have on human beings? How did the dioxin get into the waters of the Baltic Sea? Questions such as these cause students to examine the negative environmental conditions developing in the world today.

Environmentally related issues such as energy, health, and nutrition, and their relationships to the environment, are important topics for global education. These issues can be presented in classrooms at any grade level. In the early grades learning to care for plants, grow gardens, plant trees, and care for small classroom pets can be useful in environmental education. In the upper grades, analysis of chemical pollution and pollution's effect on human life is an appropriate curricular topic. Environmental education is important because it teaches that the quality of life for human beings is intimately connected to how healthy and robust the natural environment is.

THE ENVIRONMENT

What is the environment? The biosphere includes the earth's atmosphere, soil, water, and living organisms. In essence, it is everything we see and experience around us. The three elements of life support in the biosphere are the atmosphere, water, and soil. The atmosphere is the gaseous mixture that protects the earth from the excessive heat and ultraviolet radiation from the sun; it enables life on earth to exist. Water, essential to all forms of life, is distributed on the earth in a variety of forms. Salt water oceans make up 97% of the water on the earth. Ice comprises 2%. Fresh water found in rivers, lakes, the soil, and the atmosphere accounts for 1% of the water on the planet (Smith, 1996). Soil, the last of the biosphere life supports, is the material on which terrestrial life lives and maintains itself. All life on earth, including human, is dependent on these elements. For example, plants use water, carbon dioxide from the atmosphere, and sunlight to convert raw materials into carbohydrates by using the process called photosynthesis (Morgan, 1995). Animal life is dependent on plant life for its subsistence, and this pattern forms the food chain.

In the earth's history numerous changes, such as the Ice Age, occurred in the environment. Through these changes climates varied significantly, affecting life forms. As the environment changed, some life forms diminished; others that could adapt emerged. During the Ice Age, ice sheets covered much of North America and Europe and then receded. Since that period in the earth's history, the earth's environment has remained rather stable and maintained its equilibrium (Smith, 1996).

Human beings developed rather late in the earth's history. Given their ability to reason, humans have influenced the natural environment more than any other species. How did they impact the environment? If we consider that early humans sustained themselves by hunting and gathering food, their initial impact was as a part of the food chain. How did they differ from animals in their impact on the environment? The answer lies in the consumption of energy sources. Humans have always used elements of nature for their own purposes and have sometimes affected the environment in detrimental ways.

ENERGY SOURCES AND THE ENVIRONMENT

All life on earth needs energy to sustain itself. The most important source of energy is the sun. Its heat warms the earth to maintain temperatures conducive to life. The sun's energy also produces winds that affect the distribution of warmth across the globe. For example, temperatures are much higher along the equator than they are nearer to the poles. These varying temperatures create winds that affect climate and weather conditions. Energy from the sun controls the water cycle, as well, by evaporating water into the atmosphere (Spurgeon, 1988). Finally, solar energy enables plants to produce their own food. Animals do not have the ability to produce their own food and depend on plant life for their survival. Where do human beings fit into this food chain? What part do they play?

The food chain, or food web, can be easily described by levels of consumption. It begins with plant life, which produces its own food using sources in the environment. The next level of consumption is composed of primary consumers, or herbivores. These animals sustain their energy by feeding on plant life. Next in line are the secondary consumers who feed on the primary consumers and therefore are carnivorous. Tertiary consumers feed on primary and secondary consumers and/or plants; human beings belong to this category.

Decomposers, such as bacteria, fungi, and insects, live by consuming dead plants and animals and converting the dead material into minerals and organic matter for plant life to use again. (Spurgeon, 1988). Teachers can help students understand the food chain in a variety of ways. Having students create charts or graphs of the food chain allows them to visualize the food cycle and understand the interdependence of the food web. Asking students to research the role that insects play in the food chain shows students the interdependence of different species of life.

Soil Erosion: The First Effect of Human Activity

Humans first affected the environment when hunting was replaced with the domestication of animals and gathering led to the domestication of plants and the planting of crops. In time, natural vegetation was cleared to plant crops, or it was used for animal grazing. Over-grazed or over-farmed plots eventually led to soil erosion on that land.

Soil erosion is not just a problem of the past but is a current environmental problem. Activities such as the destruction of trees, over-grazing, or intensive farming leave topsoil exposed to be either blown or washed away (Spurgeon, 1988). Humans and other life forms depend on this soil for their food supply. The world has already lost between one fifth to one third of its cropland to soil erosion—this is posing a huge threat to the world's food supply (Smith, 1996). It is estimated that 20 billion tons of topsoil are lost each year to erosion. The most affected areas are in China, India, the United States, and the former Soviet Union (Morgan, 1995). Many underdeveloped nations in the world use slash and burn techniques to clear land for farming. This process kills all vegetation on the land and leaves nothing to prevent rainfall from washing away topsoil. In turn, this practice reduces the slashed and burned land to a barren plot that later cannot support crops. Consequently, slash and burn agriculture may produce food in the short term but can mortgage the future of farming in developing nations.

The availability of good soil for the food supply is also affected by the use of prime cropland for industry, and highways. The United States has used 2.7 million acres of potential farmland for uses other than farming (Smith, 1996). Presenting this information to students can prompt many questions: How can people farm and not create soil erosion? How can people graze their animals and not cause soil erosion? How can we help people in underdeveloped countries find better ways to farm their land? How can we ensure that fertile farmland is used for food production?

Encouraging students to explore possible solutions to these questions will allow them to develop an appreciation for the issues and develop a sense of environmental responsibility. They may discover, for example, that planting trees and hedges around or between rows of crops breaks the wind and reduces soil erosion. They may discover that organic farming (that uses excess plant wastes and animal wastes as fertilizers instead of chemical fertilizers) and rotating crops can be viable alternatives to chemical fertilizers. They may discover that planning is often the simplest solution to serious problems.

Deforestation: The Second Effect

The discovery of fire was a major development that accelerated human impact on nature. Fire for early humans was an energy source that provided warmth and light. Widespread use of fire began to affect virgin forests. Slash and burn agriculture uses fire as a means to clear natural vegetation. When this process is not properly managed, it can lead to significant deforestation. Deforestation is the process of clearing trees and forests for fuel, timber, or farmland.

Today human beings do not use wood for fuel alone. Wood is also used in the production of paper, buildings, and furniture. Students should be encouraged to explore the amount of time it takes for a tree to reach maturity and how deforestation affects climate and the environment in order to understand the impact of forests on human life.

There are three types of forests on earth. Each plays a role in the biosphere. Coniferous forests are indigenous to colder climates and home to cone-bearing trees such as the pine, cedar, and spruce. The species native to these forests are characterized by needles instead of leaves, and their seeds are produced in cones (Spurgeon, 1988). These forests provide homes to animals such as wolves, chipmunks, moose, and other hibernating animals.

Deciduous forests are found in milder temperatures where there is plenty of rainfall. Trees such as the oak, beech, and maple comprise these forests, and their major characteristic is the shedding of their leaves once a year. The large branches of the trees native to these forests furnish habitats for many animals, such as birds and squirrels. Their yearly leaf shedding, along with the work of the many decomposers that inhabit these forests, create a fertile soil that allows for an abundance of other plant life to grow (Spurgeon, 1988).

The last type of forest is the rainforest. Rainforests are primarily located around or near the equator. They are in areas where temperatures are consistently very warm and rainfall is constant. They are phenomenal ecosystems that contain an abundance of resources. Although they only cover 10% of the earth's land, they contain 50–70% of the earth's plant and animal species (Spurgeon, 1988). Because of their role in water, oxygen, and carbon cycles, rainforests have an impact on the regulation of the world's climate and are an important source of foods and medicines. It is estimated that there are some 1,650 rainforest plants that can be used for human consumption (Spurgeon, 1988). By 1990, more than 50% of the earth's rainforests had been eradicated (Morgan, 1995). It is estimated that every few minutes one half square mile of rainforest (or one million acres per week) is eliminated (Spurgeon, 1988).

Lessons about the importance of forests and the life forests sustain can be introduced into classrooms at all grade levels. Early elementary classes can approach the topic of forests by learning about forest animals and what happens to them when their habitats are lost. Older elementary students can examine the plant and animal life that is affected by deforestation. Middle school students can research the resources available in the forests and how they can be used to benefit humanity. High school students are able to analyze the impact deforestation has had on the chemical balance of the atmosphere and how this has affected climatic conditions. Aside from discussing the impact the loss of forests has across the globe, teachers can ask students to explore the particular effect this change has had on the indigenous peoples who depend on forests for their survival. In Brazil, for example, the Native American population has decreased "from 5 million to 200,000 over the last 400 years" (Spurgeon, 1988).

Fossil Fuels: Their Impact on the Environment

As rapid technological advances and population increases occurred, the impact humans had on the environment became more troublesome. With the Industrial Revolution came the widespread use of numerous mineral resources and fossil fuels such as coal, gas, and oil. The use of fossil fuels is needed for development in the modern world, but that progress has also had its price. Its impact on the environment has been significant. As a result, human beings began to alter the quality of the atmosphere and fresh water. Global warming and acid rain are both results of fossil fuel consumption.

The burning of fossil fuels creates an increase of carbon dioxide in the atmosphere. Carbon dioxide in the atmosphere plays an important role in keeping the earth warm because it captures the sun's heat. This process is called the "greenhouse effect" (Spurgeon, 1988). Any increase in the amount of carbon dioxide in the atmosphere can have serious consequences on the earth's temperature. Trees and other forms of plant life help to regulate the amount of carbon dioxide in the atmosphere by using the carbon dioxide for food production; therefore, deforestation plays a role in the level of carbon dioxide in the atmosphere. In the last 100 years, the amount of carbon dioxide in the atmosphere has increased from 260 parts per million to 350 parts per million (Smith, 1996). Since 1890, the earth's average temperature has increased by approximately one degree centigrade, and scientists predict that by the middle of the twenty-first century the temperature could become three to eight degrees warmer (Morgan, 1995). This global warming threatens to melt the polar ice caps; this will raise sea levels and flood coastal lands. It will also cause major changes in the climate that will alter natural vegetation and the food supply (Spurgeon, 1988).

Fossil fuel energy consumption creates another polluting problem for the environment. Cars and power plants are the two largest sources of fossil fuel consumption. Some fossil fuels emit sulfur dioxide and nitrogen oxide as they are burned. These by-products, when mixed with sunlight, oxidants, and moisture, create sulfuric and nitric acids (Smith, 1996). These acids join the water cycle and are absorbed into the atmosphere. They are then returned to the earth in the form of rainfall called acid rain (Spurgeon, 1988). Acid rain deteriorates metals and erodes stone. It can alter or kill plant life as well as acidify water sources that, in severe cases, have killed fish populations. In some parts of North America and Europe the acid level in the rainfall is equal to that of vinegar (Smith, 1996).

How should the issue of acid rain be addressed in the classroom? Younger students can explore the effects of acid rain by conducting hands-on projects, such as soaking substances in vinegar and observing the changes that occur. They could also search their communities for signs of acid rain corrosion of buildings and/or monuments. A teacher could have older students explore laws requiring emission testing for automobiles in the United States. An extensive look at laws passed by other countries to control air pollution would provide a larger picture of the problem and potential solutions.

Nuclear Energy and Its Effects

In an attempt to seek other energy sources, the atom was harnessed to produce energy. Nuclear energy uses radioactive uranium and produces energy when atomic nuclei are split ("Nuclear Energy," 1996). The environmental problems with this form of energy are the radiation hazards that arise in the nuclear fuel cycle. The process of splitting atoms creates tremendous heat, which is why nuclear power plants are equipped with cooling systems. The basic process takes place in the power plants and is relatively safe. The greatest threat, however, is a nuclear accident. In the event of a malfunction and the loss of the cooling system, a "meltdown" could occur that would release radioactive material into the environment, producing devastating effects. Two such accidents have already occurred.

In 1979, at the Three Mile Island plant in Harrisburg, Pennsylvania, a maintenance error and defective valve caused the cooling system to fail. The nuclear power reactor did shut itself down, but a human error caused the emergency cooling system to shut off. This resulted in severe damage and the escape of small quantities of radioactive gases (Kruschke, 1990, p. 94). The incident caused great anxiety for residents living near Three Mile Island and expenses of over one billion dollars ("Nuclear Energy," 1996).

Another nuclear accident occurred on April 26, 1986, at the Chernobyl nuclear plant in what was then the Soviet Union. One of the four reactors exploded and burned, due to an unapproved test run by the operators. Reports reveal that there were two explosions. The first blew the reactor's top off, and the second ignited the core, which then burned uncontrollably at temperatures of 1500 degrees centigrade (2800 degrees fahrenheit). The results of this accident were devastating. People in the area were exposed to radioactive levels 50 times greater than those generated by the Three Mile Island accident. Radioactive "fallout" spread westward to Scandinavia and other areas of northern Europe ("Nuclear energy," 1996). Over 100,000 people were evacuated from their homes and 30 deaths reported as a direct result of the accident. High school teachers may want to ask students to research these two nuclear accidents to learn about what effects they had on people and the environment. (Blix, 1989, pp. 198–203; O'Neil, 1989, pp. 62–65).

In the United States the Three Mile Island incident led to legislation requiring the Nuclear Regulatory Commission to employ strict standards for building new plants, and utility companies were required to help state and local governments with emergency programs in the event of an accident. These new standards posed financial difficulties to many companies and many projects already begun were discontinued. This, coupled with increasing costs to complete some plants according to the new standards, created an additional $100 billion cost to the U.S. economy ("Nuclear energy," 1996).

Other countries have also taken measures to ensure public safety. Sweden has limited to 10 the number of reactors it will allow. Austria has eliminated its electricity generating nuclear program. France, Japan, and Great Britain are actively continuing their nuclear power generating programs. In France, three fourths of the power is derived from nuclear power plants (Encarta, 1996). Both middle school and high school students could explore and present a worldwide comparison of the use and regulation of nuclear energy.

Another major impact that nuclear energy has on the environment is the creation of radioactive waste. This waste must be stored carefully. In the United States, for example, the desert of Nevada has been designated as a burial ground for nuclear wastes. The waste remains toxic for a period of 700 to one million years. Currently, nuclear wastes are turned into stable compounds and placed in glass or ceramic containers. These are then sealed in stainless steel drums and buried underground in geologically stable areas; their "resting places" are said to be permanent, but the drums are still retrievable. For now, the process is relatively safe; however, it is difficult to guarantee that the radioactive wastes will not leak and expose future generations to dangerous levels of radioactive materials (Meeks & Drummond 1990, pp. 116–120).

Chemical Wastes and Pesticides

Not only has industrialization caused a need for new energy sources, but it has also produced chemical by-products and industrial chemicals that can pollute the environment. Some of the most troublesome offenders are industrial chemicals called chlorofluorocarbons, or CFCs. These CFCs are used primarily in air conditioning systems, refrigeration, packing materials, aerosol sprays, and cleaning solvents (Morgan, 1995). A chemical by-product of CFCs, chlorine, attacks the ozone layer. High up in the earth's atmosphere there is a gaseous layer of ozone approximately 25 miles thick. This layer acts as a buffer and prevents the sun's harmful ultraviolet rays from penetrating the environment (Smith, 1996). Without it, no life would survive on the planet. In 1985, a growing ozone hole was discovered above Antarctica. It was found that 50% of the ozone was dissipating from Antarctica every fall, causing a hole which would close again in the spring. By 1997, the ozone hole was as large as the United States (Morgan, 1995). Many nations stopped allowing the use of CFCs by the end of the twentieth century. Unfortunately, CFCs can remain in the atmosphere for as many as 100 years; therefore, even with measures taken to ensure the termination of CFCs, their damaging effects will continue for many decades (Bailey, 1992).

Most synthetically produced pesticides also have negative side effects on the environment. They are generally insoluble in water; they adhere to plant tissue; and they can accumulate in the mud of rivers and streams. They are also resistant to biodegradable breakdown. Consequently, pesticides have entered the world's food chain. Plant eaters ingest pesticides through contaminated plants. Many fish and other aquatic animals absorb pesticides through their skin. They have been found in high concentration in the tissues of land animals. For example, pesticides affect the calcium metabolism of some birds. Their reproductive process becomes less effective, because they lack the proper calcium levels to produce eggs with shells hard enough to protect their interior. Therefore, many large predatory and fish-eating birds have come close to extinction. While pesticides can cause great harm to plant and animal life, insects have grown resistant to them.

Pesticides, along with other industrial chemicals, have managed to pollute portions of the earth's water, soil, and food supply. It is estimated that 20% of the world's urban populations and 75% of the world's rural populations have drinking water that is contaminated. In many places, including areas of the United States, water supplies contain toxic chemicals and nitrates. Water-borne diseases take the lives of some 10 million people and incapacitate approximately one third of human life in the world each year.

What can be done to protect the environment from such pollution? What have individual countries done to address the issue? What might other alternatives to the use of these chemicals be? Encouraging students to look into such problems and explore possible solutions is an important task for teachers. Planting garlic or marigolds around crops to act as an insect deterrent is a method used by organic farmers; this practice suggests that there are some solutions to problems with low environmental impact. Students can evaluate energy forms, such as solar energy and windmills, that are currently being used to produce electricity. Activities such as these help students think about the environment and social responsibility (Buchholz, 1993, pp. 231–270).

HOW HAS THE WORLD ADDRESSED ENVIRONMENTAL ISSUES?

In the United States, the destruction of the environment has been an issue since the 1860s. In 1864, George Perkins Marsh wrote *Man and Nature,* a book in which he addressed the impact humans had on the environment and then advocated that affected areas be left alone to recuperate naturally or be restored through alterations. Many U.S. citizens have played a part in the preservation of the environment. Teachers can have students research the lives of John Muir (founder of the Sierra Club), John James Audubon, John Chapman (Johnny Appleseed), Henry Wood Elliot, John Burroughs, Rachel Carson (whose works link pollution to human health), and many others.

In 1970, the U.S. Congress founded the Environmental Protection Agency (EPA). The EPA is an independent government agency whose responsibility is to protect and conserve the environment for future generations. Its primary aim is to manage and eliminate air and water pollution, as well as the pollution caused by radiation, pesticides, and other toxic substances. It has enforced standards emanating from the following laws:

- *The Clean Air Act* provides limits to air polluting emissions.
- *The Clean Water Act* provides water pollution limits for industries and municipalities.
- *The Wilderness Act* identifies and protects designated forest lands and wilderness areas.
- *The Endangered Species Act* commands the protection and restoration of endangered wildlife (Hoyle, 1993 pp. 3–32).

Teachers of all grade levels can use these acts as teaching tools to present environmental issues. Elementary teachers can make use of the Endangered Species Act and the Wilderness Act to discuss animals and plants that are being protected as well as how many species have been saved and/or destroyed since these two pieces of legislation were enacted. Middle and high school teachers can examine the Clean Air Act and the Clean Water Act to discover with their students the standards established for air and water pollution and the consequences of any violations of these standards. Classes can also explore the effectiveness of these acts. In addition, students can research private organizations that have been involved in the preservation of the environment, such as the National Wildlife Federation, Greenpeace, the Wilderness Club, Friends of the Earth, and the Sierra Club, to discover what these groups' efforts have accomplished. Students can also explore the arguments of groups that have opposed these environmental organizations.

It is important for students to known that environmental education is a worldwide issue. In 1970, Congress enacted the Environmental Education Act, which provided funding for teacher training and community education programs (PL 91–516). In 1975, the United Nations also began a program to promote environmental education on a global scale.

The United Nations held a conference on the environment and global development in 1992, known commonly as the "Earth Summit." It met for 12 days just outside Rio de Janeiro, Brazil, and was attended by representatives of 178 nations. This conference declared that the preservation of the environment is the world's first priority. Two documents were created: Agenda 21 was a 900 page plan for environmental development, and the Rio Declaration is a six-page document for integrating economic development with environmental issues (Smith, 1996; United Nations Department of Public Information, 1994). These documents were to serve as the framework for global action in reversing the negative trends of environmental degradation. In spite of these domestic and global efforts to address the environment, the future health of the world environment remains questionable if action is not taken.

HEALTH AND NUTRITION

All human life is dependent upon a variety of substances found in the environment. These elements are food, non-food substances, and food nutrients. Non-food substances include oxygen and water. Food nutrients include carbohydrates, proteins, fats, vitamins, and minerals (Nelson, 1988). The lack of any of these substances can cause ill health, disease, or death to an individual. Consequently, human health is directly related to the availability of clean air, clean water, and healthy nutrients; a healthy environment is essential to life.

In order to appreciate the importance of having a healthy environment, it is necessary to understand the role that air, water, and nutrition play in supporting human life. Teachers can present this material with varying degrees of complexity depending on the ages of their students. Bulletin boards can provide graphic illustrations and enhance a classroom discussion of nutrients. Teachers and students can also create charts and food pyramids to illustrate the importance of the different life supporting substances.

Oxygen is one of the most important substances for humans. The human body uses this essential substance to oxygenate its cells and tissues; through the process of respiration, blood is purified and oxygenated and then carries the oxygen throughout the body to tissue and organs. In one day, an average adult male will inhale approximately 700,000 cubic inches of air and purify 125 barrels of blood in his lungs (Nelson, 1988). Without oxygen, the human body will experience brain damage and/or death within a very short period of time.

Water is also essential to human life. It composes 55–60% of an adult's body weight (Whitney, 1996). In cells it provides a medium in which chemical reactions can occur. Outside the cells it acts as a transporting agent for the body to help wash away wastes. It also helps to regulate and maintain body temperature (Thomas, 1973) The human body loses water through the kidneys, bowels, lungs, and skin and needs to constantly replenish its water supply (Nelson, 1988). A lack of water, or dehydration, can prevent essential body functions from occurring. Dehydration can be life threatening.

The human body uses energy to maintain its activity and to regulate body temperature. There are three nutrients that play a major role in energy production: proteins, carbohydrates, and lipids, or fats. Proteins are very important to the human body. The word *protein* is derived form the Greek *protos,* which means "first" (Thomas, 1973). Proteins are first because they are fundamental for growth and for building and repairing tissue in the body. As they are oxidized in the body, they also produce energy and heat (Thomas, 1973). A deficiency of protein produces an energy malnutrition called *kwashiarkor.* This malnutrition produces great weakness and is marked by a loss of body fat and wasting of muscle (Latham, 1996b).

Carbohydrates are the fuel for metabolism. They are easily converted into glucose, which is burned during the metabolic process and produces life sustaining energy (Latham, 1996c). There are two types of carbohydrates: simple and complex. Simple carbohydrates are sugars found in fruits and vegetables and are easily absorbed without great digestive activity. Complex carbohydrates must first be converted into simple sugars in order to be absorbed. They require heat and greater digestion before they are useful to the human body (Nelson, 1988). Fats, or lipids, are an added source of energy to the human body. They produce twice as much energy as carbohydrates and can easily be stored for use when carbohydrates are not present. There are two types of fats: saturated and unsaturated. Saturated fats come from animal sources, are solid at room temperature, and are high in cholesterol. Unsaturated fats are found in vegetable sources, are liquid at room temperature, and are lower in cholesterol (Latham, 1996c).

Vitamins and minerals are also necessary substances for human health. They are primarily obtained from vegetables and fruits. Vitamins are organic compounds that play a part in the enzyme system fortifying the metabolism of proteins, carbohydrates, and fats (Latham, 1996c). There are fat-soluble vitamins such as A, D, E, and

K and water-soluble ones, such as C and all the B-complex vitamins. Vitamin deficiencies cause many diseases (see Figure 5.1).

Minerals are inorganic compounds also important to human health. They are necessary for the structural composition of hard and soft body tissue and are used in enzyme systems, muscle contractions, nerve reactions, and blood clotting (Latham, 1996c). The body needs major and trace minerals. Major minerals include calcium and iron. Some examples of trace minerals are copper, zinc, and iodine. Both types of minerals are important, and deficiencies can have adverse effects on human health. A lack of iron causes anemia. A lack of iodine during pregnancy can cause mental retardation in the child (Latham, 1996c).

Another significant issue is the quantity of nutrients needed to maintain good health. In the United States the amount is calculated by specifying an ideal daily allowance. The Food and Nutrition Board of the National Research Council of the National Academy of Science is the organization responsible for setting the Recommended Daily Allowances (RDA) (Whitney, 1996). The RDA designates the daily amounts of proteins, carbohydrates, fats, vitamins, and minerals needed for humans to grow and maintain good health. Figure 5.2 shows examples of minimum daily requirements.

How do individuals throughout the world meet these requirements? This is an issue that the teacher of global issues can explore with students to better understand the state of world health. Teachers can begin by presenting the global efforts of the issue, such as by using the United Nations Universal Declaration of Human Rights

FIGURE 5.1   Vitamin Deficiency Chart

Vitamin	Deficiency Effect
A	Causes blindness in children
D	Causes rickets, a disease that creates skeletal deformities
C	Causes scurvy, a disease which affects the gums, skin, mucous membranes, and causes swelling of the joints
B-complex	Can cause beriberi, a disease that affects the nervous system and is manifested by severe sweating and a rapid heartbeat
B-complex	Can cause pellagra, a disease that produces insomnia, indigestion, diarrhea, headache, and vertigo

Adapted from Latham, M. (1996b). Malnutrition [CD-ROM]. *Microsoft Encarta '96 Encyclopedia.* Funk & Wagnalls.

FIGURE 5.2   U.S. RDA and World Health Organization Nutrient Intake Recommendation

NUTRIENT	U.S. RDA[1] MEN	U.S. RDA WOMEN	WHO[2] MEN	WHO WOMEN
Protein (g)	45	45	37	29
Vitamin A	1,000 (RE)[3]	800 (RE)	750 (g)	750 (g)
Vitamin D	400 (IU)[4]	400 (IU)	2.5 (mg)	2.5(mg)
Thiamin (mg)	1.4	1.0	1.2	.9
Riboflavin (mg) B2	1.7	1.5	1.8	1.3
Niacin (mg)	18	13	19.8	14.5
Folic Acid (mg)	0.4	0.4	200	200
Vitamin B12 (mg)	6	6	2	2
Vitamin C (mg)	60	55	30	30
Calcium (g)	0.8	0.8	0.4–0.5	0.4–0.5
Iron (mg)	10	18	5–9	14–28

1 RDA: Recommended Daily Allowance

2 WHO: World Health Organization

3 RE: Retinal Equivalent, a measure of vitamin A activity

4 IU: Independent Units

Adapted from Smolin, L., & Grosvenor, M. (1994). *Nutrition: Science and applications.* Fort Worth, TX: Saunders College Publishing, cover page; and Whitney, E. N., Nunnelley Hamilton, E.M., & Rady Rolfes, S. (1996). *Understanding Nutrition* (7th ed.). St. Paul, MN: West.

(see Figure 5.3). This document was adopted by the UN Commission on Human Rights in 1948. It is not a legally binding document; rather, it is a statement of UN charter members' intent to "promise to take both separate and joint actions to promote universal respect for and observance of human rights" (O'Brien, 1996).

Article 25 of this document states that individuals "have the right to whatever they need so that they do not fall ill, do not go hungry, have clothing and have a home" (O'Brien, 1996). Also established by the United Nations in 1948 was the World Health Organization (WHO). The primary responsibility of this body is helping all peoples achieve the "highest levels of health" ("World Health Organization," 1996). In a 1978 international conference,

FIGURE 5.3   The Universal Declaration of Human Rights

Whereas recognition of the inherent dignity and of the equal and inalienable rights of all members of the human family is the foundation of freedom, justice and peace in the world,

Whereas disregard and contempt for human rights have resulted in barbarous acts which have outraged the conscience of mankind, and the advent of a world in which human beings shall enjoy freedom of speech and belief and freedom from fear and want has been proclaimed as the highest aspiration of the common people,

Whereas it is essential, if man is not to be compelled to have recourse, as a last resort, to rebellion against tyranny and oppression, that human rights should be protected by the rule of law,

Whereas it is essential to promote the development of friendly relations between nations,

Whereas the peoples of the United Nations have in the Charter reaffirmed their faith in fundamental human rights, in the dignity and worth of the human person and in the equal rights of men and women and have determined to promote social progress and better standards of life in larger freedom,

Whereas Member States have pledged themselves to achieve, in co-operation with the United Nations, the promotion of universal respect for and observance of human rights and fundamental freedoms,

Whereas a common understanding of these rights and freedoms is of the greatest importance for the full realization of this pledge,

Now, therefore,

The General Assembly

Proclaims this **Universal Declaration of Human Rights** as a common standard of achievement for all peoples and all nations, to the end that every individual and every organ of society, keeping this Declaration constantly in mind, shall strive by teaching and education to promote respect for these rights and freedoms and by progressive measures, national and international, to secure their universal and effective recognition and observance, both among the peoples of Member States themselves and among the peoples of territories under their jurisdiction.

Article 1
All human beings are born free and equal in dignity and rights. They are endowed with reason and conscience and should act towards one another in a spirit of brotherhood.

Article 2
Everyone is entitled to all the rights and freedoms set forth in this Declaration, without distinction of any kind, such as race, colour, sex, language, religion, political or other opinion, national or social origin, property, birth or other status.

FIGURE 5.3 *Continued*

Furthermore, no distinction shall be made on the basis of the political, juris-dictional or international status of the country or territory to which a person belongs, whether it be independent, trust, non-self-governing or under any other limitation of sovereignty.

Article 3
Everyone has the right to life, liberty and the security of person.

Article 4
No one shall be held in slavery or servitude; slavery and the slave trade shall be prohibited in all their forms.

Article 5
No one shall be subjected to torture or to cruel, inhuman or degrading treat-ment or punishment.

Article 6
Everyone has the right to recognition everywhere as a person before the law.

Article 7
All are equal before the law and are entitled without any discrimination to equal protection of the law. All are entitled to equal protection against any dis-crimination in violation of this Declaration and against any incitement to such discrimination.

Article 8
Everyone has the right to an effective remedy by the competent national tri-bunals for acts violating the fundamental rights granted him by the constitu-tion or by law.

Article 9
No one shall be subjected to arbitrary arrest, detention or exile.

Article 10
Everyone is entitled in full equality to a fair and public hearing by an indepen-dent and impartial tribunal, in the determination of his rights and obligations and of any criminal charge against him.

Article 11
1. Everyone charged with a penal offence has the right to be presumed inno-cent until proven guilty according to law in a public trial at which he has had all the guarantees necessary for his defence.
2. No one shall be held guilty of any penal offence on account of any act or omission which did not constitute a penal offence, under national or interna-tional law, at the time when it was committed. Nor shall a heavier penalty be imposed than the one that was applicable at the time the penal offence was committed.

Article 12
No one shall be subjected to arbitrary interference with his privacy, family, home or correspondence, nor to attacks upon his honour and reputation.

(continued)

FIGURE 5.3 *Continued*

Everyone has the right to the protection of the law against such interference or attacks.

Article 13
1. Everyone has the right to freedom of movement and residence within the borders of each State.
2. Everyone has the right to leave any country, including his own, and to return to his country.

Article 14
1. Everyone has the right to seek and to enjoy in other countries asylum from persecution.
2. This right may not be invoked in the case of prosecutions genuinely arising from non-political crimes or from acts contrary to the purposes and principles of the United Nations.

Article 15
1. Everyone has the right to a nationality.
2. No one shall be arbitrarily deprived of his nationality nor denied the right to change his nationality.

Article 16
1. Men and women of full age, without any limitation due to race, nationality or religion, have the right to marry and to found a family. They are entitled to equal rights as to marriage, during marriage and at its dissolution.
2. Marriage shall be entered into only with the free and full consent of the intending spouses.
3. The family is the natural and fundamental group unit of society and is entitled to protection by society and the State.

Article 17
1. Everyone has the right to own property alone as well as in association with others.
2. No one shall be arbitrarily deprived of his property.

Article 18
Everyone has the right to freedom of thought, conscience and religion; this right includes freedom to change his religion or belief, and freedom, either alone or in community with others and in public or private, to manifest his religion or belief in teaching, practice, worship and observance.

Article 19
Everyone has the right to freedom of opinion and expression; this right includes freedom to hold opinions without interference and to seek, receive and impart information and ideas through any media and regardless of frontiers.

Article 20
1. Everyone has the right to freedom of peaceful assembly and association.
2. No one may be compelled to belong to an association.

FIGURE 5.3 *Continued*

Article 21
1. Everyone has the right to take part in the government of his country, directly or through freely chosen representatives.
2. Everyone has the right of equal access to public service in his country.
3. The will of the people shall be the basis of the authority of government; this will shall be expressed in periodic and genuine elections which shall be by universal and equal suffrage and shall be held by secret vote or by equivalent free voting procedures.

Article 22
Everyone, as a member of society, has the right to social security and is entitled to realization, through national effort and international co-operation and in accordance with the organization and resources of each State, of the economic, social and cultural rights indispensable for his dignity and the free development of his personality.

Article 23
1. Everyone has the right to work, to free choice of employment, to just and favourable conditions of work and to protection against unemployment.
2. Everyone, without any discrimination, has the right to equal pay for equal work.
3. Everyone who works has the right to just and favourable remuneration ensuring for himself and his family an existence worthy of human dignity, and supplemented, if necessary, by other means of social protection.
4. Everyone has the right to form and to join trade unions for the protection of his interests.

Article 24
Everyone has the right to rest and leisure, including reasonable limitation of working hours and periodic holidays with pay.

Article 25
1. Everyone has the right to a standard of living adequate for the health and well-being of himself and of his family, including food, clothing, housing and medical care and necessary social services, and the right to security in the event of unemployment, sickness, disability, widowhood, old age or other lack of livelihood in circumstances beyond his control.
2. Motherhood and childhood are entitled to special care and assistance. All children, whether born in or out of wedlock, shall enjoy the same social protection.

Article 26
1. Everyone has the right to education. Education shall be free, at least in the elementary and fundamental stages. Elementary education shall be compulsory. Technical and professional education shall be made generally available and higher education shall be equally accessible to all on the basis of merit.

(continued)

FIGURE 5.3   *Continued*

2. Education shall be directed to the full development of the human personality and to the strengthening of respect for human rights and fundamental
freedoms. It shall promote understanding, tolerance and friendship among all
nations, racial or religious groups, and shall further the activities of the United
Nations for the maintenance of peace.
3. Parents have a prior right to choose the kind of education that shall be giv-
en to their children.

Article 27
1. Everyone has the right freely to participate in the cultural life of the community, to enjoy the arts and to share in scientific advancement and its benefits.
2. Everyone has the right to the protection of the moral and material interests
resulting from any scientific, literary or artistic production of which he is the
author.

Article 28
Everyone is entitled to a social and international order in which the rights and
freedoms set forth in this Declaration can be fully realized.

Article 29
1. Everyone has duties to the community in which alone the free and full development of his personality is possible.
2. In the exercise of his rights and freedoms, everyone shall be subject only to
such limitations as are determined by law solely for the purpose of securing
due recognition and respect for the rights and freedoms of others and of meeting the just requirements of morality, public order and the general welfare in
a democratic society.
3. These rights and freedoms may in no case be exercised contrary to the purposes and principles of the United Nations.

Article 30
Nothing in this Declaration may be interpreted as implying for any State,
group or person any right to engage in any activity or to perform any act
aimed at the destruction of any of the rights and freedoms set forth herein.

---

the WHO announced that the goal should be "health for every human being without distinction of race, religion, political belief, economic or social condition by the year 2000" (Taubert, 1988). How
has the health and nutrition of the world fared since 1948 and
1978? How has the world responded to this document?

In 1996 the *World Health Report* stated that up to half of the
world's population is at risk of getting many endemic diseases, and

infectious diseases are the world's chief causes of death. These diseases victimize some 17 million people each year, the majority of whom are children (WHO, 1997). Poverty endangers the lives of hundreds of millions of people throughout the world; these people often suffer from malnutrition that weakens the body and increases the likelihood of disease.

Almost half of the world's population suffers from diseases attributed to insufficient or contaminated water supplies. WHO reports that diarrheal diseases resulted in three million deaths in 1995. Eighty percent of these fatalities were children under age five (WHO, 1997). Typhoid fever afflicts some 16 million persons and kills approximately 600,000 persons each year. It is estimated that 79 million people are at risk for cholera in Africa (WHO, 1997). The WHO states that there are about 40 million cases worldwide of intestinal parasitic infections attributed to contaminated water supplies (WHO, 1997). Food-borne diseases also play a major role in people's health. Salmonellae, campylobacter, and listeria are just a few of the bacteria that can inflict food-borne diseases. In the United States alone, it is estimated that there are between 6.5 million and 80 million cases of food-borne diseases each year (WHO, 1997).

Historically, famine has occurred in many parts of the world. Famine comes from the Latin word for hunger (Latham 1996a). It is caused by both natural disasters such as drought and by human factors such as war. Malnutrition also causes serious health problems. Initially, the lack of nutrition causes weight loss. By cutting nutrient intake by one half, an individual can reduce body weight by one fourth (Latham, 1996a). Additional drops in nutritional levels can result in serious disease and/or starvation. In children, the effects are more devastating. Children can suffer permanent physical or brain damage by receiving low levels of nutrition from which an adult could recover. The WHO estimates reveal that in developing nations across the globe at least 600 million people suffer from malnutrition (Latham, 1996b), and between 5 and 20 million people die of starvation each year (Latham, 1996b). It is estimated by U.S. nutritionists that 10 million children in the United States currently suffer malnutrition in the form of anemia, obesity, and undernutrition (Latham, 1996b).

Teachers and students can learn the world's response to hunger and malnutrition by exploring the works of organizations such as

WHO, the United Nations Children's Fund (UNICEF), and the United Nations Food and Agricultural Organization (FAO). Students can be made aware of hunger by learning about the homeless in their own communities as well as abroad. Inviting an individual who works with the homeless or at a missionary, or a Peace Corps volunteer, to speak to students can help the students to understand and develop empathy toward people suffering from malnutrition and hunger. Teachers can involve students in hunger relief projects by collecting food for homeless shelters and food kitchens (older students can be asked to volunteer in such facilities) or by raising money to send to UNICEF to sponsor a foster child somewhere in the world. Middle and high school students can research the work of Bob Geldof and Live Aid (the concert performed to raise funds for relief in Ethiopia), as well as the pop music community's response to the famine in Ethiopia in the 1980s. Young adults might be interested to discover that in a six month period Bob Geldof and Band Aid provided Ethiopia with the following:

- 6 trucks
- 22 Land Rovers
- 8 Land Cruisers
- 18 water tanker trailers
- 23 hospital tents
- 140 tons of high energy biscuits
- 1,240 tons of dried skim milk powder
- 25 tons of full cream milk powder
- 2 tons of whole milk
- 52 tons of medical supplies
- 7 freezers
- 510 tons of vegetable oil
- 450 tons of sugar
- 1,000 tons of grain
- 10 tons of cooking and eating utensils (Arneson, 1985)

Students can learn that they can make a difference. They should be challenged to examine the problems the world faces and how important the environment is to the health and well being of the people of the world. As Carl Sagan has eloquently stated,

There are worlds on which life has never arisen. There are worlds that have been charred and ruined by cosmic catastrophes. We are fortunate: we are alive, we are powerful; the welfare of our civilization and our species is in our hands. If we do not speak for Earth, who will? If we are not committed to our own survival, who will be? (Provensen, 1995, p. 31)

SUMMARY

Human survival depends on an increased respect for the environment. Our lives are related to and dependent on all life on earth. Students in the global classroom, therefore, should examine environmental issues from bio-centric and anthropocentric perspectives. They can then contrast these two perspectives. The role of teachers is to help students understand the importance of all life forms and develop a sense of responsibility for the environment.

Using the three basic elements of the environment, students can study the impact humans have made on the biosphere and how important it is to address environmental issues. The atmosphere and water are the two elements on which all life is in some way dependent. Soil is equally important to all terrestrial life. A close examination of the earth's history will reveal to students that the actions of human beings have altered the earth's environment more than any other factor.

As societies moved from hunting and gathering to domesticating plant and animal life, the first negative environmental impacts by humans occurred. Clearing, planting, and over-grazing caused soil erosion, a problem still prevalent today. Soil erosion leaves once-fertile land barren and affects food supplies. Planting the same crop year after year will deplete minerals in the land. Crop rotations can often be a simple solution to this problem.

The discovery of fire by humans was a development that especially affected the environment. As wood became a resource for human life, deforestation became a problem. While trees provide wood for fire, housing, furniture, and paper for humans, deforestation affects many life forms that inhabit the forests of the world. A close examination of the depletion of the rainforests of the world will define for students the environmental problems deforestation creates for the animals, plants, and people who inhabit these areas.

With the Industrial Revolution came the use of new mineral resources and also fossil fuels. These energy forms were more efficient than burning wood and paved the way for the use of machines and high levels of fossil fuel consumption. The burning of these fuels emits increased levels of carbon dioxide into the atmosphere. This can have serious effects on the earth's temperature. Since the 1890s, the greenhouse effect has caused the earth's temperature to increase approximately by one degree centigrade.

Fossil fuels burned in machines such as automobiles emit sulfur dioxide and nitrogen oxide as they are burned. The acids are absorbed into the atmosphere and returned to the earth in the form of acid rain. Acid rain deteriorates metals and erodes stone. Its effects have been devastating to many life forms.

In an attempt to find more environmentally safe forms of energy, people developed nuclear energy. Splitting atoms is a relatively environmentally safe form of energy. The major disadvantage of this form of energy is the possible threat of a nuclear reactor meltdown; nuclear reactors produce great heat and require a cooling system. A meltdown could release radioactive material into the environment, which would have devastating results. The Chernobyl accident, in which a nuclear reactor exploded and burned, is an excellent example for students to explore in order to understand the benefits and dangers of nuclear energy.

Industry produces many waste products that negatively affect the environment. Many polluting chemicals are dumped into bodies of water or placed in landfills. Plants and animals are greatly affected. The use of chlorofluorocarbons (CFCs), found in aerosol cans, refrigeration units, and cleaning solvents, produces a by-product of chlorine that attacks the ozone layer. The ozone layer is vital to life on earth and acts as a buffer to protect the earth from the sun's ultraviolet rays. In 1985 a growing hole in the ozone layer was discovered above Antarctica.

Pesticides are generally harmful to living things. They are usually not water-soluble. They adhere to plant and animal life and can cause disease. Their resistance to biodegradable breakdown makes them likely to enter and stay in the food chain. Some large predatory and fish-eating birds have come close to extinction because pesticides have altered calcium metabolism, which ultimately affects the reproductive process. Unfortunately, pesticides have devastating effects on various life forms, and the targeted insects often grow immune to pesticides' effects.

Students should be made aware of the efforts of individuals like George Perkins Marsh, James Audubon, Rachel Carson, and many others who played their part in preserving the environment. The Environmental Protection Agency and the Earth Summit are other topics that students can research to discover the efforts made by their government and the world at large to protect the environment. The global classroom should emphasize the responsibility each student has to protect the earth and life upon it.

Relating environmental problems to the health and well-being of humans can help students address the issues. Human health is directly related to the availability of clean water, clean air, and healthy nutrients. The World Health Organization estimates show that at least 600 million people in the world suffer from malnutrition, and between 5 and 20 million people die of starvation each year.

Asking students to explore mineral and vitamin deficiencies, water-borne and food-borne diseases, and the number of people affected by them can illustrate the urgency of the state of the world's health. According to the 1996 *World Health Report* of the UN World Health Organization, almost half the world's population suffers from diseases attributed to the lack of, or contamination of, water supplies (WHO, 1997). There were, and are, millions of deaths as a result of diseases and infections that could be eliminated simply by drinking clean water, both in the United States and the world. Students should be aware of the magnitude of such diseases.

A look at UNICEF, the United Nations Food and Agricultural Organization, and the works of groups of individuals will show students the efforts made to ensure the health and well-being of the people of the world. Involving students in service projects, such as a feeding program or foster child sponsorship, can initiate a sense of responsibility. In the global classroom students can and need to learn that they can make a difference in the world.

SUGGESTED ACTIVITIES

Elementary

Objectives

- To learn the concepts of endangerment and extinction.
- To understand the importance of habitat on survival.
- To appreciate human responsibility for the care of nature.
- To learn and use the concept of personification.

Activity

Introduce students to the concepts of endangerment and extinction. What do they mean, and how do they affect life on earth? (Using dinosaurs is a great way to illustrate the concept of extinction.) Depending on the age of students, provide them with or have them research endangered animals around the world. Ask students to look into questions about the causes of the animals' endangerment: What role do changes in animals' habitats play? What role have humans played in the problem? Who determines and/or how is determination of endangerment made? What actions have been taken to protect these animals? How close is the animal to extinction? How can people prevent this animal from becoming extinct?

Follow-up

Have students prepare an oral presentation of the information they obtained. The students should provide a visual representation of the animal they researched. Have them share a two minute oral report of the information, from the perspective of the animal. (They should personify the voice of the endangered animal.) Allow time for an exchange of questions and answers between students in the class and the "animal." Provide a world map in the classroom to allow students to mark on the map where their animal lives. An extension to this activity can include hosting an endangered species fair for the entire school, creating masks or costumes to be worn during the presentations, and writing stories about the endangered animals. Service projects, such as caring for a class pet or raising funds to sponsor an endangered animal, can also help students develop a sense of environmental responsibility.

Middle School

Objectives

- To be fully aware of the impact modernization has had on indigenous peoples in various parts of the world and times in history.
- To learn about the lifestyles of indigenous peoples.
- To realize how environmental changes affect the lifestyle of indigenous peoples.
- To appreciate the role dominant cultures have played in the dislocation and/or demise of indigenous peoples.
- To understand the relationship between the environment and culture.

Activity

Assign each student to a group. Have each group research indigenous groups in the United States, such as the Cherokees, the Navahos, and the Winnebagos. Other students could research Mayans in Mexico, indigenous groups from the rainforests of Brazil, the Aborigines of Australia, and the Zulu of South Africa. Ask the students to look into their group's assigned history, its way of life, and the impact of the environment on its culture. What resources from the environment did/do the groups use for survival? What plant and animal life did/does the group depend on? How did/does modernization change lifestyles and threaten existence? What happened to the resources the group depended on for survival? How have deforestation, soil erosion, and pollution affected the group's population and way of life? What is the economic condition of the group now (if applicable)? How has the world responded to the needs of these people? If available, Internet access can be a helpful tool to gather current information. Have students keep a journal of their thoughts and feelings on the information they gather when addressing the previous questions.

Have each group give an in-depth report on the indigenous peoples they researched. They could present their findings using a talk show format in which a host can mediate discussion between members of the indigenous group and colonizers or industrialists who influence their lives and environment. This can be followed by questions from the classroom audience. Another suggestion is to make a mock video documentary of the indigenous group in which

an anthropologist can visit and speak with the members of the indigenous group and report on the changes in their lives caused by
changes in their environment.

Follow-up
On a world map, mark the points where the indigenous groups
live(d). Have the class discuss how the by-products of modernization
have created problems for these people. Ask the class how they feel
about the problems discussed and raise some possible solutions.

High School

Objectives

- To identify ecological problems faced by nations.
- To contrast the ecological problems faced by other nations to
  those found in the United States.
- To recognize the interdependence of people around the globe
  and the relationship of ecological problems to the future of the
  planet.

Activity
Ask students to identify some ecological problems. Ask them to research a particular problem, such as deforestation or water pollution, in many different nations. Have them detail the scientific
changes that these problems produce in the environment. How
have these problems affected human growth and development?
Have these problems affected people's lives? What actions have been
taken to correct or prevent these problems? The students should
write a report and create a chart illustrating the impact their topic
has had on the environment, and then share their resources with
the class.

Follow up
Have students compare and contrast ecological problems from
across the globe. Ask them to consider the role they can play in addressing the problems. Have them discuss global efforts to alleviate
or control environmental concerns. Allow them time to brainstorm
about possible solutions.

QUESTIONS FOR REFLECTION

1. Are present trends of population growth, health problems, and environmental destruction sustainable? Why or why not?

2. What are some of the ways in which governments, international bodies, organizations, and individuals have acted to protect the environment and the health and well-being of people around the globe? How effective do you think these have been in solving problems? What would you propose as a better or more efficient way to deal with problems?

3. How are hunger and poverty related? Can they be eliminated? What are their causes? How urgent do you feel these problems are?

4. Of the following methods for increasing food production, which do you feel are viable options? Why?

   • clearing forests
   • irrigating arid lands
   • increasing yields of farmland already in production
   • developing new crops through biotechnological agriculture

5. Research the *World Health Reports* published by the World Health Organization over the last 10 years and evaluate the statistics. Have there been improvements in the state of the world's health? How many cases of disease and death could have been prevented in your opinion? How effective do you think policies and programs already instituted have been in decreasing the number of people affected by disease over the last 10 years? What do you propose could be done to improve the state of the world's health?

REFERENCES

Arneson, D. (1985). *Live aid.* New York: Modern.

Bailey, R. (1992, June). The hole story: The science behind the scare. *Reason, 24*(2).

Blix, H. (1989, December). Nuclear power and the environment. *Environmental Policy and Law, 19*(6).

Buchholz, A. R. (1993). *Principles of environmental management.* Englewood Cliffs, NJ: Prentice-Hall.

Environmental Education Act. (PL 91–516). 95th United States Congress, 2nd Session, Vol. 34, p. 636 (1978). Washington, DC: Congressional Quarterly, Inc.

Environmental Encyclopedia. (1994). Detroit, MI: Gale Research.

Harms, V. (1994). *Almanac of the environment.* New York: Grosset & Putnam.

Hoyle, R. (1993). *Gale environmental almanac.* Detroit, MI: Gale Research.

Kruschke, R. E., & Jackson, B. M. (1990). *Nuclear energy policy.* Santa Barbara, CA: ABC-Clio.

Latham, M. (1996a). Famine [CD-ROM]. *Microsoft Encarta '96 Encyclopedia.* Funk & Wagnalls.

Latham, M. (1996b). Malnutrition [CD-ROM]. *Microsoft Encarta '96 Encyclopedia.* Funk & Wagnalls.

Latham, M. (1996c). Nutrition, human [CD-ROM]. *Microsoft Encarta '96 Encyclopedia.* Funk & Wagnalls.

Marsh, G. P. (1871). *Man and nature; or physical geography as modified by human action.* New York: Scribner.

Meeks, F., & Drummonds, J. (1990, June 11). The greenest form of power. *Forbes, 145*(12).

Morgan, S. (1995). *Ecology and environment: The cycles of life.* New York: Oxford University.

Nelson, D. (1988). *Maximizing your nutrition.* Santa Cruz, CA: Author.

Nuclear energy [CD-ROM]. (1996). *Microsoft Encarta '96 Encyclopedia.* Funk & Wagnalls.

O'Brien, E. (1996). *Human rights for all.* St. Paul, MN: West.

O'Neil, B. (1989, June 24). Nuclear safety after Chernobyl. *New Scientist, 122*(1670).

Provensen, A. (1995). *My fellow Americans.* San Diego: Browndeer.

Smith, R. (1996). Environment [CD-ROM]. *Microsoft Encarta '96 Encyclopedia.* Funk & Wagnalls.

Smolin, L., & Grosvenor, M. (1994). *Nutrition: Science and applications.* Fort Worth, TX: Saunders College.

Spurgeon, R. (1988). *Ecology: Usborne science and experiments.* London: Usborne.

Taubert, S. E. (1988). The bio-environment and education. In A. Vlavianos-Arvanitis (Ed.), *Biopolitics: The bio-environment.* Athens, Greece: Biopolitics Organization.

Thomas, C. L. (Ed.). (1973). *Taber's cyclopedic medical dictionary.* Philadelphia: F. A. Davis.

United Nations Department of Public Information. (1994). *Agenda 21: The United Nations Programme of Action from Rio.* New York: United Nations.

United Nations General Assembly. (1948, December 10). *Universal declaration of human rights.* Minneapolis, MN: Human Rights USA Resource Center.

Wallerstein, I. M. (1977). *Rural economy in modern world-society. Studies in comparative international development: Studies in comparative international development* (Vol. 12, No. 1). New Brunswick, NJ: Transaction periodicals consortium.

Whitney, E. N. (1996). *Understanding nutrition* (7th ed.). St. Paul, MN: West.

Whitney, E. N., Nunnelley Hamilton, E. M., & Rady Rolfes, S. (1990). *Understanding nutrition.* St. Paul, MN: West.

World Health Organization [CD-ROM]. (1996). *Microsoft Encarta '96 Encyclopedia.* Funk & Wagnalls.

World Health Organization. (1997, February 3). Executive summary. *The world health report 1996.* Available:
<www.who.ch/whr/1996/exsume.htm>

6

GLOBAL ISSUES: GLOBAL ECONOMICS AND GLOBAL SECURITY

Major Points

- The world has become a global marketplace where goods and services are exchanged and technologies have improved the conditions for this to occur.

- Economics involves the transformation of resources into goods and services that satisfy human needs and wants.

- The clarification of the different types of economic resources is important to an understanding of global security.

- The workings of an economic market are crucial for comprehending global economic hegemony.

- Land, labor, capital, and entrepreneurial ability are the four basic categories into which resources are divided.

- Supply and demand are the basic forces that affect prices in capitalist economies.

- The economies of nations can be described as capitalist, socialist, or mixed.

- Governments try to influence fluctuations in economic cycles.

The authors wish to acknowledge the assistance of Victoria Samaras Polentas with the preparation of this chapter.

- World systems theory states that all of the world's nations participate to some degree in a global economy.
- The World Trade Organization governs agreements concerning the trade of products and copyrighted material.

Economics provides an obvious global link for students in the United States to identify with people in other parts of the world. It is simple to illustrate the interdependence of our society and the rest of the world. Our markets are saturated with products from other countries. In our grocery stores, there are numerous fruits and vegetables with stickers, tags, or signs indicating different countries of origin. In our department stores there are toys, appliances, clothing, and many other items with tags or labels saying, "Made in..." On our streets, there are numerous imported automobiles. As we look around us, we can identify that U.S. citizens have a definite economic link to other nations. On the surface, the link seems obvious and can easily be viewed as simple trade; however, the global economic link between the United States and other nations goes far beyond simple trade. Our economies are interdependent and deeply intertwined. To better understand these relationships, it is necessary to examine basic economics and economic systems.

THE BASIC COMPONENTS OF ECONOMICS

Economics is defined as the social science that studies how people work to transform resources into goods and services to satisfy their needs and wants, as well as how people distribute the goods and services (Gottheil, 1995). Consider a hunting and gathering society of the past. Some individuals hunted animals, and foods were gathered by other individuals. Hunters and gathers would decide how the product (food) would be distributed among themselves.

This concept can be introduced to students in a variety of ways. Students can participate in a hands-on project by producing a product (such as cookies) from a variety of resources (milk, eggs, flour) and then determining how the cookies should be distributed among the members of the class. This would enable the students to understand the basics of economics. Once this basic concept is introduced, a discussion of resources can ensue: What are resources? Where do they come from? How are they used?

Resources are the "inputs" people use to produce goods and services (McEachern, 1997). Land, labor, capital, and entrepreneurial ability are the four basic categories of resources. Land can contain a wide array of resources. The amount of land, although important, is not the major factor that determines its usefulness. Other factors such as water sources, plant life, animal life, minerals, oil reserves, and other such "gifts of nature" play a major role in the "richness" of the land (McEachern, 1997). Students at any age level can explore the land resources in their own communities and compare them to those of other communities or nations. For example, the land resources of the Great Plains states vary greatly from those of Florida, Egypt, or India.

Labor is the resource of human activity. It includes both a physical and an intellectual component. In essence, labor is human effort (Gottheil, 1995). Physical labor would include the activities of a farmer, mechanic, or others whose work involves active physical effort. Intellectual labor would include the endeavors of an engineer, lawyer, professor, or others whose work is comprised primarily of mental effort. Labor is dependent on another very important resource: time. The "raw material of life" is a description that has been given to time (McEachern, 1997). Individuals can distribute their time; they can "sell" their time as labor or they can "spend" their time in leisure activities. This idea can be explained to students in terms of their own schoolwork. By asking simple questions such as, "What happens if you don't do your homework or if you don't study for a test?" Students can discover that they will not be "compensated" with a good grade without applying their intellectual labor.

Labor resources are extremely important. Without them, other resources would not be economically viable. An orange growing on a tree cannot become a food product except through the farmer's effort. The orange tree is cared for and then the orange is picked and sent to market for purchase and consumption. The farmer's labor converted the orange (a land resource) into a food product that can then be distributed to fulfill a human need. To illustrate this point, tell students that if an essay were assigned and no one in the class did it (labor resource), then there would be no papers (products) for the teacher to consume.

Capital resources are the inventions of humans that enable the production of goods and services. They are divided into two categories: physical capital and human capital (McEachern, 1997). Physical capital encompasses items such as machines, transportation systems, buildings, or tools that help in the production of goods and the delivery of services. For example, the bus driver's bus, the doctor's stethoscope, and the plumber's wrench are all physical capital resources. Human capital refers to the skills and knowledge that individuals attain to improve themselves as labor resources. The bus driver's knowledge of a city's streets or the doctor's knowledge of human anatomy and medicines are examples of human capital. Teachers can ask students to create a chart of physical and human capital resources such as the one in Figure 6.1.

The last resource, entrepreneurial ability, is more abstract. It involves the ingenuity to think of new products and services that will be needed and taking a risk to produce them. New products and services do not simply emerge. Someone creates them and takes the chance to produce, market, and sell them. Older students can be asked to create products they think will be needed and construct marketing campaigns to present these new products to their classmates. Students often enjoy this type of project and are able to appreciate the concept of entrepreneurship as well as each other's creative abilities.

Students may confuse human capital with this entrepreneurial ability. One way to clarify the difference is to explain that human capital is involved with an established good or service. Entrepre-

FIGURE 6.1   Capital

Physical Capital

Item	Used for	Used By
Bus	Transporting people	Bus driver
Blow torch	Fusing metals	Welder

Human Capital

Item	Used for	Used by
Knowledge of human anatomy and medicines	Curing illness and comforting pain	Doctor

neurial ability is the creative process that conceives of new goods and services or designs more profitable ways of producing or delivering an already established good or service. For example, when a doctor performs surgery, his human capital enables him to do his job. When the same doctor develops a new way of doing a surgical procedure that creates less risk to the patient or requires less recovery time, then the doctor is applying entrepreneurial ability.

It is important to clarify the meaning of goods and services. Goods are the tangible products produced that are used to satisfy human need and want. An orange, a designer dress, and a new automobile are all goods. Services, on the other hand, are intangible activities that are performed to fulfill a need or want. A concert performance, for example, is an activity that fulfills a want for entertainment. A haircut is a service because it fills the need for good grooming.

Economics focuses on how humans work to provide goods and services as well as how these goods and services are distributed. To understand the distribution process, it is important to identify where the distribution occurs and how it is determined. For example, a hunting and gathering society typically divides its food by the number of people who need to eat. In contemporary societies, most of the distribution of goods and services occurs within a market. Individuals come to the market as both buyers and sellers. They come to purchase a good or a service, or they come to the market with a good or service to sell. At the market, there is a system of exchange, usually of a monetary nature. The exchange is based on the notion of equal value: that is, the money paid is proportional to the value of a good or service received. Value is determined by supply and demand: that is, goods and services that are in great supply and have low demand are of lesser value than those that are scarce but for which there is great demand. Scarcity is an insufficient supply that cannot meet the demands of the populace.

Although somewhat abstract, the concept of supply and demand is one that can be illustrated even for young children. A teacher could, for example, pass out a picture of a giraffe and ask the students to color the picture. The teacher could then distribute a brown crayon to every child and a yellow crayon to only three children in the class. The students would all need to use the yellow crayon to color their giraffe picture, but only three would be available. The yellow crayons would become a scarce good. Because all students have a brown crayon, their supply meets the demand of the market. The yellow crayon becomes more valuable than the brown crayon, because it is in demand.

Older students can often identify with this concept when they are reminded that items such as designer clothing, concert tickets, or new music releases are often sold out before they have had a chance to purchase the items. Using the example of concert or sports event tickets, a teacher could ask a class of high school students the following: What happens to the price of tickets if they are resold after an event is sold out? What is scalping? Why does it occur? Answers to these questions can initiate a discussion of marketplace supply and demand.

Economic Systems

Having established the basic components of economics, it is important to focus on how decisions about the production of goods, the delivery of services, and the distribution of both goods and services is made. In the social sciences, the term *economy* is defined as the social institution that determines what will be produced, how it will be produced, and who will receive it (Billings, 1991, pp. 63–76). By examining the development of societies throughout the world and their economies, one can see how the production and distribution of goods and services differ.

Two U.S. sociologists, Gerhard and Jean Lenski, (Lenski, Nolan, & Lenski, 1995) have created a model that illustrates the development of societies as they responded to technological innovations. They explain that there are four types of societies: the hunting and gathering society, the horticultural and pastoral society, the agrarian society, and the industrial society (Cockerham, 1995). Figure 6.2 illustrates the process and development according to the Lenskis.

Consider the members of these societies. Members of each of the groups are the labor resources. Their environment is the land resourse. The technology available to them and their abilities to use it are capital, and the new technology that emerges is the entrepreneurial ability.

If we follow the development of farming, the initial entrepreneurial skill would be the discovery of the ability to domesticate plant and animal life. The next step would be the creation of the

FIGURE 6.2   The Lenskis' Model Applied to Agriculture

Resource	Hunting and Gathering	Horticultural and/or Pastoral	Agrarian	Industrial
Land	plants/animals	plants/animals	plants/animals	plants/animals
Labor	human	human	human/animal	human
Capital	human	hoe	plow	tractor
Entrepreneurial	domestication of plants and animals the invention of the hoe	production of a surplus; trade begins; concept of property and wealth; invention of the horse drawn plow	greater production of surplus; greater wealth; more extensive trade; banking begins; discovery of fossil fuels; invention of the machine; invention of the tractor	formation of agribusiness

Adapted from Cockerham, W. (1995). *The global society: An introduction to sociology.* New York: McGraw-Hill, pp. 131–136.

hoe, which made preparing the soil for planting quicker and less laborious. This was followed by the creation of the horse-drawn plow. This invention allowed more time (another resource) for other products and services to be created by making farming more efficient. A plow could prepare six lanes for planting at one time. Using a hoe would have required six people, each preparing one lane.

With the discovery of fossil fuels (a land resource) and the invention of the tractor, the horse-drawn plow was replaced with the tractor. This increased the amount of land that could be plowed. The result was greater food production in less time. This technological development continued to the present with the use of ultra-modern farming equipment.

The Lenskis' model provides a clear picture of how entrepreneurial ability affected the development of the social structure and the economy. Using food production as a model, in hunting and gathering societies individuals had a relatively equal status. The hunters and gatherers were equally important in producing food for the group. If the hunters came home empty handed, they ate food the gatherers had collected. When the supply was a bit greater than the demand, or vice versa, the group developed a mechanism to decide how food would be distributed. In the pastoral and/or horticultural stage, the idea of ownership emerges. The interdependence among people for survival lessens, and individuals begin to accumulate property. Early trade began to provide groups a variety of foodstuffs. Nomadic pastoral groups could have traded food products with stationary agricultural communities. Consequently, a market emerged and with it, supply and demand.

Individuals who did not own their own land or herds of animals would not be able to participate in the market as well as an individual who owned these things. This, coupled with new technology that allowed for faster production, created an inequality of wealth. These events may have led to the creation of a new economic system in the agrarian stage—feudalism. In feudalism, a few individuals owned most of the land. Others who did not worked for the owners (or lords) in exchange for a very small portion of the product. In the twentieth century, according to the Lenskis' model, the use of fossil fuels hastened the onset of the Industrial Revolution and the industrial stage.

Capitalism is the theory of an economic system in which resources are privately owned. The owners (capitalists) employ labor and resources to create products to be sold in the market. The purpose of the capitalist is to produce products that will generate a profit. Profit is the capitalist's total revenue from the sale of products, minus the costs of resources (McEachern, 1997). The capitalist often uses profit to reinvest in more resources, which will create more products. Capitalism generates cycles, and each cycle should be larger than the previous one if more resources are added. Figure 6.3 shows how the increase of wealth occurs in this economic system.

Capitalism resembles feudalism because many resources are owned by relatively few individuals (i.e., 0.5% of the U.S. population annually earns at least one million dollars [U.S. Bureau of the Census, 1996]). It differs from feudalism because workers no longer work for a portion of the product, but rather for a wage. This wage is offered in return for labor from workers who help produce a product or service. For example, General Motors may hire a welder to weld parts of an automobile, or a farmer may hire a farm hand to help harvest a crop. The welder would not receive an automobile in return for his work, nor would the farm hand receive any part of the harvest. Both would be paid a wage that they could use in the market to purchase goods.

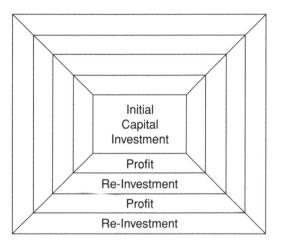

Initial
Capital
Investment

Profit

Re-Investment

Profit

Re-Investment

FIGURE 6.3   The Growth of Capital

In theory, under pure capitalism, the owners of the resources could also affect economic activity through pricing. Theoretically, they could set any price for their products in a market free of regulation (McEachern, 1997). However, if prices are too high for most consumers to buy, demand falls and prices must be lowered. The nature of capitalism, depending on conditions in world and domestic markets, also carries the potential for instability. The 1929 crash of the stock market in the United States and the German economic crisis in the late 1920s and early 1930s are good examples of the capitalist system's possibility for—albeit rare—extreme turmoil. Nations attempt to regulate markets to keep major fluctuations from occurring.

In the United States, the national government performs this function. For example, in 1971 President Nixon ordered a price and wage freeze to help stabilize the economy (McEachern, 1997). President Reagan ordered striking air traffic controllers back to work in 1981; Reagan felt that a strike by the Professional Air Traffic Controllers Organization would create an economic disaster (McEachern, 1997). The national government makes trade agreements, policies, and treaties. It is the government that sets minimum wage requirements, price ceilings (maximum legal prices), and price floors (minimum legal prices). The Federal Reserve Board controls the cost of credit and the money supply. These controls are adjusted according to the state of the economy.

Socialism is the theory of an economic system that was envisioned after the start of the Industrial Revolution in response to the capitalist system. In this type of economy, the resources are publicly owned and labor is supposed to have input into the production and distribution of goods and services. Karl Marx, the founder of socialism, believed that the capitalists (bourgeoisie) exploited the workers (proletariat) (Cockerham, 1995). He thought that exploitation, which he attributed to the generation of profit, would eventually lead to revolt and the formation of a new, more equitable economic system. The new system would be communism, in which property and wealth would be communally shared. Socialism was considered by Marx to be a transitional stage during which a newly established socialist government would still be necessary to control production and distribution before the society could enter communism. His thinking influenced many social movements in the world, and many nations had revolutions that centralized their economic activity into the hands of the government. The former Soviet Union, China, and Cuba are examples of nations in which this occurred.

The mixed economy contains both capitalistic and socialistic components (Cockerham, 1995). In essence, some of the economic activities are privately owned while others are publicly owned. Usually, the publicly owned sectors in such economies include transportation, education, and health care. Private industries produce nearly all goods in nations with the mixed economy, or democratic socialism. Nations that adopt democratic socialism do not experience social revolution, nor is a new government created. The Scandinavian countries and France are good examples of democratic socialism.

Economic Activity and the World Systems Theory

There are many different economies in the world today. There are still hunting and gathering peoples as well as horticultural and/or pastoral, agrarian, socialist, capitalist, and democratic socialist societies. However, the economic system that is preeminent in the world is capitalism, and all economies interact with it (Cockerham, 1995). In order to understand the present global economic circumstances, it is necessary to appreciate the movement of capital across national boundaries.

Most economies have three basic sectors: the primary, secondary, and tertiary (Cockerham, 1995). The primary sector yields raw materials from nature. For example, most food products that are planted, harvested, and consumed—with little, if any, processing—would be part of the primary sector. The secondary sector transforms raw materials into finished products. Automobiles and furniture are examples of the products created in this sector. The tertiary sector of the economy is the area where services rather than goods are generated (Cockerham, 1995). Advanced capitalist societies, such as the United States and the United Kingdom, contain all three sectors; however, in these societies the largest sector is the tertiary one. In the United States, approximately 60% of the labor force works in the tertiary sector, 35% in the secondary, and only 5% in the primary (Cockerham, 1995). A developing nation will have a much higher percentage of workers in the primary sector and fewer in the secondary and tertiary sectors. Kenya, for example, has only 6.5% of its labor force in the tertiary sector, 13.5% in its secondary sector, and 80% in the primary sector (Cockerham, 1995).

A U.S. sociologist, Immanuel Wallerstein, has formulated a world system theory that defines the modern world economy as capitalistic. He explains that the world system "emerged in the sixteenth century with the expansion of Western Europe's capitalist economic system through conquest into the Americas and through extensive trade links with Eastern Europe and Asia" (Cockerham, 1995, p. 175). He suggests that capitalist expansion in search of better resources and profit potential prompted many societies to join the capitalist world economy. As a result, these host societies that did not initiate their own involvement in the world economic system were compelled to join (Cockerham, 1995). Their initiation was not on equal grounds with other nations. Dominant capitalist nations had the advantage; they already had the monetary surplus to purchase and process the resources in the host society, often leaving that society short of its own resources. This phenomenon resulted in greater development for the advanced capitalist nations and developmental delays for host nations. These societies are still in a process of catching up to the wealthier ones (Calhoun, Keller, & Light, 1997).

Wallerstein's theory goes on to explain that through history and shifts in world power, the world system that developed left a single world economy of a capitalistic nature. This world system has brought about a global division of labor (Calhoun et al., 1997). At the core are highly developed nations, in the semi-periphery are less developed nations, and in the periphery are developing nations (Cockerham, 1995). The placement of a nation in this economic world system is closely related to its reliance on each of the three economic sectors.

Nations in the core have a high percentage of their labor force in the tertiary sector, are highly industrialized, and have a high concentration of wealth. Wallerstein suggests that the core nations dominate the system because of their economic strength and great wealth. World economic powers are Japan, the United States, and the European Union (Cockerham, 1995).

Nations in the semi-periphery have a large percentage of their labor forces in the secondary sector of the economy and are competitive in the production of finished products. These products, such as automobiles and electronics, require more capital and high technology to produce, which gives them greater value in the global market than the products of the primary sector (Cockerham, 1995). Nations such as Brazil, Taiwan, and Singapore are in the semi-periphery. They are industrialized and competitive in the world market but do not have the great amount of wealth and resources to be a part of the core.

The peripheral nations are those with labor forces predominantly in the primary sector. These nations specialize in labor intensive, low technology products (Cockerham, 1995). Nations such as Kenya, India, Peru, and China are in the periphery. What is the link that ties the core, semi-periphery, and periphery together? How are they connected? Why does Wallerstein (1977) call it a world system? In order to answer these questions, it is necessary to find the place where the three can meet. This place is the market, where core, semi-peripheral, and peripheral nations all trade their goods and services.

World Trade

Trade, or the exchange of goods and services, has occurred for thousands of years. In the seventeenth and eighteenth centuries, the formation of nation–states in Europe encouraged the present form of international trade. Kings, queens, and other heads of state realized that foreign trade promoted wealth and power; it also provided countries with a greater diversity of products to consume. It was soon evident that international trade allowed a nation to specialize in the goods it could produce most efficiently and at the lowest cost. It could obtain other needed products through trade ("Foreign Trade," 1996). In 1776, the Scottish economist Adam Smith published *The Wealth of Nations*, a book in which he discussed the benefits of international trade. He suggested that nations should specialize in products that they could produce at a lower cost than their trading partners could. He believed this would lead to increased output and more efficient use of resources ("Foreign Trade," 1996). His work became the basis for the classical school of economics that was prevalent during the late eighteenth and early nineteenth centuries ("Foreign Trade," 1996).

International trade poses a variety of questions: What happens to domestic or national interests? How are goods exchanged? Is there a balance that must exist between products exported to the market and products imported from the market? International trade is a basic component of an individual nation's economy; therefore, a nation's government acts as its protecting agent. The government will usually set specifications and regulations to protect the economy as a whole. If imports threaten a specific industry, then the government may limit the importation of the product.

The two basic ways in which government can affect international trade are with quotas and tariffs. Quotas are regulations that set a maximum quantity of imported products (Gottheil, 1995). The result of quotas is usually a higher cost to the consumer because of the limited supply of that good. At the same time, quotas protect domestic producers from foreign competition ("General Agreement on Tariffs and Trade," 1996). Tariffs are taxes imposed on imported goods (Gottheil, 1995). They function to increase the price of imported items, which allows domestic producers a larger share of the market. Tariffs also provide revenue for the government. An examination of the price of imported automobiles in an automobile-producing nation will clearly illustrate this circumstance. A BMW is much more expensive in the United States than if it is purchased in Germany; a Ford Mustang is much more expensive in Germany than in the United States. Ultimately, government regulations attempt to regulate trade ("General Agreement on Tariffs and Trade," 1996).

At the beginning of the twentieth century, governments did not place equal tariffs on comparable goods. Different tariffs were levied on the products from different nations. Usually lower tariffs were given to favored nations ("General Agreement on Tariffs and Trade," 1996); therefore, trade became a source of international economic conflict, and disputes erupted among nations. Efforts were started to promote international trade policies. The first major agreement among nations was the General Agreement on Tariffs and Trade (GATT). It was signed by 23 nations at the Geneva Trade Conference in 1947 ("General Agreement on Tariffs and Trade," 1996). Members of the GATT agreed to

- treat all member nations equally with respect to trade
- reduce tariff rates through multinational negotiations
- reduce import quotas (McEachern, 1997, p. 763)

The member nations of the GATT grew to 117 by 1994 ("General Agreement on Tariffs and Trade," 1996). From its beginning, members of the GATT met for rounds of negotiations. The last round in April 1994 called for the establishment of the World Trade Organization, or WTO (McEachern, 1997).

The WTO began operations in January 1995. It currently coexists with the GATT. The GATT is an international agreement enforced by a nation's department of trade. WTO is an international organization that enforces and oversees the GATT. Eventually it will replace GATT when all GATT members transfer their memberships to WTO (McEachern, 1997). One of the areas covered by the WTO not covered by GATT is the realm of the services. The GATT was merchandise oriented. The WTO also involves services and copyrighted trade items such as books, films, and computer programs. For example, the WTO guarantees that computer programs are protected the same as literary works, and it specifies what databases are to be protected by copyright (McEachern, 1997). The major functions of the WTO include

- administering and implementing the trade agreements that compose the WTO
- acting as a forum for trade negotiations
- resolving trade disputes
- overseeing national trade policies

• cooperating with other international institutions involved in policy making for the global economy (McEachern, 1997)

Many nations participate in more than one trade organization or treaty. Throughout the world, countries that have a common bond (usually geographic proximity) have formed trade communities. In 1932, the Ottawa Agreements let preferential tariffs be levied for the nations of the British Commonwealth ("Foreign Trade," 1996). In Europe one of the largest world trading communities began in 1948 with Belgium, the Netherlands, and Luxembourg as members. In 1951, France and West Germany joined the group, and it became known as the European Coal and Steel Community (ECSC). These same nations established the European Economic Community (EEC) in 1957. In 1993, the European Economic Community became the European Union ("Foreign Trade," 1996). Communist nations also had their own trade organization called the Council for Mutual Economic Assistance (COMECON). It began in 1949 but ended when the Soviet Union dissolved ("International Monetary Fund," 1996). The North American Free Trade Agreement (NAFTA) was signed by the United States, Canada, and Mexico in 1993; its purpose was to create a free market for everything produced and consumed in the three countries (Gottheil, 1995).

How do nations exchange goods and services in the international market when each has its own currency that determines the value of its products? In a domestic market, the currency used is the same between buyer and seller. When producers from different nations meet in an international market, how is the value of exchange determined? How much would a $30 pair of jeans from the United States be worth in Japanese yen? How are currency exchanges determined and regulated? As trade and other international financial transactions increased in the twentieth century, the need to facilitate and stabilize the flow of dollars, marks, yens, pounds, and other currencies became vital. To meet this need, a number of organizations were founded. The most important organization is the International Monetary Fund (IMF), which began in 1947. Its objective is "to promote international monetary cooperation and to facilitate the expansion and balanced growth of international trade through the establishment of a multilateral system of payments and the elimination of foreign-exchange restrictions" ("International Monetary

Fund," 1996). The current membership of the IMF is 179 nations. At one time, communist countries were excluded. Today all sovereign nations, regardless of their economic systems, are eligible to join ("International Monetary Fund," 1996). China joined the IMF in 1980 (Rourke, 1997, p. 502). In April 1992, IMF accepted applications from Russia and 13 other nations of the former Soviet Union (Rourke, 1997).

As an activity, students could collect information from newspapers to compare the exchange rates of different currencies to U.S. dollars. This activity can be used for students from upper elementary to high school. Computing conversions of yens to pounds or marks to dollars can provide students with a feel for international exchange. Discussions on how and where to convert dollars into other currencies could involve a field trip to the bank or a visit from a banker. Older students could explore how international transactions occur: What happens when you charge an item with a credit card in Mexico? Is the merchant paid in U.S. dollars or Mexican pesos? Who does the conversion? Where does the actual exchange occur? How do countries and corporations calculate their exchanges? Exploring international banking systems can help older students appreciate the inner workings of the world market and the economic ties that exist among nations.

Multinational Corporations and Global Economics

Easily identifiable symbols of the global economy are multinational corporations. These corporations own and/or operate businesses in more than one country (Cockerham, 1995). Many U.S. corporations are multinational. Multinational corporations have led to globalization, the development of worldwide economic and social relationships (Cockerham, 1995). Modern technology has enabled globalization to occur by providing many new and efficient forms of communication systems. Sending or obtaining information from a company halfway around the globe can be accomplished in a matter of seconds. Asking students to brainstorm about how technology has linked the world together can illustrate this concept. Computers that are connected to networks may be used to give students direct experiences with global communications.

A close-up examination of multinational corporations can show students that the same products they buy are available to people in other countries. Using Coca-Cola as an example, students can experience the globalization of a multinational corporation. Coca-Cola is one of the most popular soft drinks in the world; its sales in the U.S. market have taken second place to its international market. Eighty percent of its revenue comes from outside of the United States (Cockerham, 1995). In its attempt to reinforce the idea of a single global market to its employees, it no longer uses the terms "domestic" and "foreign" at its corporate headquarters in Atlanta, Georgia (Cockerham, 1995). The Coca-Cola Corporation has even used a global unity theme in its advertising. "I'd like to teach the world to sing" was the theme that sent the message of a unified world drinking Coca-Cola.

The automobile industry is another area in which globalization is easily recognizable. U.S. companies such as Ford and General Motors (GM) produce and sell automobiles in the United States and Europe (Cockerham, 1995). GM produces trucks in China. Fiat, an Italian car manufacturer, assembles cars in Russia. Japanese corporations such as Toyota and Honda have assembly plants in the United States (Cockerham, 1995). The following is a clear example of the globalization and the interdependence of nations:

> When an American buys a Pontiac Le Mans from General Motors, he or she engages unwittingly in an international transaction. Of the $20,000 paid to GM, about $6,000 goes to South Korea for routine labor and assembly operations, $3,500 goes to Japan for advanced components (engines, axles, and electronics), $1,500 goes to West Germany for styling and design engineering, $800 goes to Taiwan, Singapore, and Japan for small components, $500 goes to Britain for advertising and marketing services, and about $100 to Ireland and Barbados for data processing. (Reich, 1991, p. 113).

A single so-called "American" product involves the efforts of people in nine different nations!

It is important to discuss with students the impact that multinational corporations have on the nations that host them. A multinational corporation expands to other nations seeking more resources or cheaper labor. What happens when Coca-Cola opens a plant in Greece? What happens when Wal-Mart owns a clothing manufacturing plant in Guatemala? How does the company affect the host country? How does the company influence the domestic clothing industry?

Economist Robert Gilpin suggests that the principal goal of a multinational corporation is to produce products at the lowest possible cost for the world market and optimize profit (Cockerham, 1995). He further explains that some multinational corporations are only minimally accountable to anyone in their host countries. As a result, they can take investments out, avoid taxes, and exploit the local populations by paying low wages (Cockerham, 1995). Most of the corporation's profits may go to the corporation's home country, leaving little for the host economy. While some of these corporations cultivate business, prompt economic growth, and create new jobs in the host countries, they may also curb the growth of local and domestic industry. This phenomenon is often referred to as neo-colonialism—that is, a socioeconomic domination from the outside that does not include direct governmental or political control on the inside (Cockerham, 1995).

Having older students look into the role that a multinational corporation plays in a host country's economy can be eye opening. A teenage guitar player may then be able to understand why his U.S.-made Fender Straticaster guitar is more costly than the same Fender Straticaster made in Mexico. What does the guitar company pay an employee in the United States? What does it pay a Mexican employee for the same work? How much would a Mexican guitar player pay for either the U.S. or the Mexican Straticaster guitar in Mexico? Why do companies such as Nike manufacture so many of their shoes outside the United States? How many countries now host franchises such as McDonald's? Exploring these questions can help students understand the impact of global economics and the dependencies that are created.

Multinational corporations need and depend on less developed nations for greater profit generation and resources, as well as new markets. Multinational corporations in developed nations unleash the great productivity of the capitalist economic system, which will boost economic development in that country. The less developed nations depend on multinational corporations for jobs and investments even though multinational investment often creates few jobs in poor countries and can also stifle the development of local industries. Gilpin concludes that regardless of the negative effects, for many poor nations foreign investment is better than no investment; it is the most important factor responsible for economic growth (Cockerham, 1995).

High school students can do case studies and assess the impact multinational corporations have had on a developing nation. They could weigh the positive and negative effects as if they were the governing body of that nation and decide on negotiating strategies with the corporation. This could prove to be an excellent illustration of the interdependency of nations in the global economy. Economically, no nation stands alone in today's world.

GLOBAL SECURITY

Rivalries have always been present among sovereign states. In the past, a state's effort to increase its own security by expanding military power often threatened the security of its neighboring states. International security has historically been defined primarily in terms of national survival needs. Security has meant the protection of the state, its boundaries, its people, and its values from external attack. International organizations such as the United Nations emphasize the inviolability of territorial boundaries and the prohibition of external interference by other nations into the internal affairs of a sovereign state. The emphasis of these values is intended to reduce the frequency of interstate aggression. When the threat of external aggression exists, it provides a rationale for creating powerful national military systems. It can also be used to justify policies that emphasize defense over domestic welfare and encourage measures that severely restrict citizens' rights and freedoms.

In the twenty-first century, war among nations is less likely to produce a clear winner. The world has become too small and too crowded; its people are too intermingled and interdependent; its weapons are too lethal. Ballistic missiles, long range aircraft, and weapons of mass destruction negate the security offered by distance from an enemy. Efforts made by great powers to preserve their military dominance will stimulate emerging powers to acquire increased military strength. This will prompt the great powers to reinforce their capabilities, and then a vicious cycle ensues. The result of this cycle could be a rise in political tensions, a waste of resources, and war by accident. International relations have changed and so should the nature of global security. Global security must rest on a commitment for joint survival rather than a threat of mutual destruction.

Collective security as envisaged in the UN Charter is based on the idea of UN members renouncing the use of force among themselves and pledging to defend any member who is attacked by external force. Collective security depends on the certainty of a joint military response to aggression. Comprehensive security emphasizes changing the military notion of security with cooperation, confidence building, and demilitarization. Comprehensive security is a people-centered approach. It is concerned less with weapons and more with basic human dignity. Human security includes safety from chronic threats such as hunger, disease, and repression. It is important for students to recognize the importance of a global security that encompasses the security of people as well as the more traditional notion of military security. Perhaps the following norms could be considered for global security in a new era:

- All people in all states have a right to a secure existence, and all states have an obligation to protect those rights.
- The primary goals of global security policy should be (1) to prevent conflict and war, (2) to maintain the integrity of the planet's life support systems by eliminating the economic, social, environmental, political, and military conditions that generate threats to the security of people and the planet, and (3) to anticipate and manage crises before they escalate into armed conflicts.
- Weapons of mass destruction are not considered legitimate instruments for national defense.
- The production and trade of arms should be controlled by an international community.
- The development of military capabilities beyond those required for national defense and for support of UN action should be considered a potential threat to world security.

Embracing these norms would go a long way toward responding to the most pressing security challenge of the twenty-first century: preserving and extending the progress made in securing states against the threat of war, while finding ways to safeguard the rights and dignity of individuals.

SUMMARY

The world has developed into a complex economic system in which nations are economically interdependent. Many students use products and services that originate in other nations. By pointing out international economic activity, teachers can help students become aware of their ties with people around the world. Through the study of economics, teachers and students can explore the production and distribution of goods and services that fulfill their needs. All goods and services come from a variety of resources; land, labor, capital, and entrepreneurial ability are resources that work to create the goods and services available in the market for consumption. Someone picked the orange one eats, made the car one drives, learned to heal one's wounds, and created the video games one plays.

Societies have developed from simple hunting and gathering communities to industrial nations. Each developmental stage has included new technologies that enhanced the production of goods and services. Once people began to produce a surplus of what they needed, the concepts of property and wealth emerged. Trade became a vital instrument for the distribution of the surplus. The development of trade created markets. As markets developed and more and more goods and services were available, an exchange value was necessary. Banking emerged, and money was created. Inherent in the market is the notion of supply and demand; Goods and/or services that fill the needs of the market are more valuable than those that do not.

A variety of economic systems emerged that address the ways in which goods and services can be produced and distributed. The basic economic structures are feudalism, capitalism, socialism, and democratic socialism. Each economy has three sectors: the primary, secondary, and tertiary. The primary sector involves taking products from nature, such as food items. The secondary sector involves transforming natural resources into finished products. The tertiary sector involves the delivery of services, such as banking. World systems theory places nations of the world into the categories of core, semi-periphery, and periphery, determined by the nation's primary form of economic production. Countries with high percentages of workers in the tertiary sector are considered core nations. Countries with high percentages in the secondary sector are in the semi-periphery. Developing nations, whose workers are mainly in the primary sector, are in the periphery of the world system.

A world system economy based on capitalism requires a means to provide an exchange value for the variety of currencies involved in international trade that helps to maintain world economic order. The response to this need emerged as the General Agreement of Tariffs and Trade (GATT) and later the World Trade Organization (WTO). The GATT focused primarily on goods and the WTO evolved to develop regulation of services. The International Monetary Fund was created to regulate monetary exchange rates and transactions.

Multinational corporations are the vehicles that help to influence global economics. Historically nations have participated, sometimes without consent, in the world capitalist economy. Colonialism and neo-colonialism have played a significant role in bringing developing nations into the world market. Multinational corporations provide jobs and investment to many nations; however, they can also hinder domestic economic development by consuming resources and monopolizing markets.

The global economy today is based on a capitalist economic system in which core nations have the highest concentration of wealth. It is important that the global classroom provide an atmosphere in which students can explore global economic forces and appreciate the role they play as consumers and producers of goods and services.

Global security is of major importance. It involves the prevention of warfare and preservation of the environment, as well as the protection of the people of the world from hunger, disease, and repression. The world is beginning to look at security issues from global and regional perspectives as well as from the viewpoint of individual nations. Ultimately, if more of the basic needs of people are met, the world will become a safer place for all of its citizens.

SUGGESTED ACTIVITIES

Elementary

Objective

- To appreciate the international market.
- To develop the concept of a product or good in the marketplace.
- To understand the workings of a market.

Activity

Have the students collect an array of products or goods and bring them in to class. Create a classroom chart of the products that addresses the following: the item, its cost at the market, the place it was made (grown or produced), the students' demand for it, and the item's availability.

Follow-up

Discuss the results on the chart. What is the relationship between the items' costs and their availability? Why or why not is a particular item in demand? How many items are grown or produced in other countries? How many are produced domestically? For products that are not domestically produced ask students, "Do you think this product is available to the children who live in the country it comes from? Do you think that the products made in the United States are available to those children as well?"

Middle School

Objectives

- To understand the exchange values of different currencies.
- To convert other currencies into U.S. dollars.
- To convert U.S. prices into other currencies.
- To compose a friendly letter.
- To use the Internet (if available).

Activity

Have students gather information from a variety of sources (such as banks, newspapers, and the Internet) on the current exchange rates of various international currencies. Ask students to calculate conversions: How many Japanese yen are there in 10 U.S. dollars? Repeat this exercise over several weeks, months, or the entire school year in order for students to see the variation that can occur in exchange values.

Next, have the students in the class write to pen pals in countries of their choice. In the course of their correspondence, students should ask their pen pals about the costs of products such as Nike athletic shoes, Levi's jeans, McDonald's burgers, and Coca-Cola. Are the products available to the pen pal? If so, what is the cost for them in the other country? Does the pen pal's country produce its own version of athletic shoes, jeans, burgers, or cola products, and what is the price of the domestically produced item? When the students receive responses, have them share the information with the class. Ask them to convert the prices of the items into U.S. dollars for better comparison. Keep a log of responses. (This activity may also be done on the Internet if this is available to students.)

Follow-up
Compare the values of different currencies to U.S. dollars and the change in value over time. Ask students to speculate on the causes of the variations. Contrast the costs of products in different nations. How much does a Coke cost in Peru? Mexico? Japan? Ask students to look up per capita incomes and minimum wages for the countries of their pen pals and to compare the costs of these products to the number of hours one needs to work in order to buy the products.

High School

Objectives

- To comprehend the concept of neo-colonialism.
- To analyze the functions of a multinational corporation.
- To evaluate the positive and negative impacts multinational corporations have on their host countries.
- To understand a nation's place in world systems theory.

Activity
Have the students define the following terms: neo-colonialism, multinational corporations, and world systems theory. Ask the students to research a multinational corporation and one of the nations in which it does business. Students should prepare an oral presentation and include the following information about the multinational corporation:

- percentage of its sales that are domestic and foreign
- the number of countries in which the corporation does business
- the amount of investments made in the host country researched

- the number of jobs the corporation has provided to the host country
- availability of their products in the host nation's market

Students should also present the following information about the host country:

- What percentage of its workers are in the primary, secondary, and tertiary sectors of the economy?
- What place does this nation have in the world system theory?
- What is the per capita income?
- What is the nation's currency, and what is the currency's value in U.S. dollars?
- What benefits has the nation derived from the multinational corporation?
- Have there been any negative consequences from the multinational corporation's activities?

Follow-up

Ask students to evaluate the information they obtained and to compare it to the concept of neo-colonialism. Do they think it applies to the nation they studied? Why or why not?

QUESTIONS FOR REFLECTION

1. How are goods and services produced, delivered, and distributed in your society? Is there an equal distribution? Explore these issues in the context of feudalistic, capitalist, socialist, and democratic socialist economic systems.

2. Using the notion of supply and demand, analyze which goods in your society have greater or lesser value. Evaluate their scarcity. Explore the reasons why these goods and services are or are not scarce and why their costs vary.

3. Identify nations you would define as being in the core, semi-periphery, and periphery of the world's economy. Look at the breakdown of jobs in these nations. What are these nations' places in the world economic system? To what degree are multinational corporations a part of these nations' economies?

4. Discuss the International Monetary Fund's functions. How are monetary exchange rates determined and affected? How could the rates affect your vacation plans to travel abroad? How might exchange rates affect an individual from a peripheral nation who planned to travel to the United States or an individual from the semi-periphery visiting Japan?

5. What impact does a multinational corporation have on a host nation in the developing world? How is this impact different from the same multinational corporation operating in a developed host nation? Discuss the presence of Coca-Cola and McDonald's in nations of the world. Could the presence of these products in other nations affect not only their economies but their cultures as well? If so, how?

REFERENCES

Balance of payments [CD-ROM]. (1996). *Microsoft Encarta '96 Encyclopedia.* Microsoft Corporation.

Billings, H. (1991). *Economics, principles, and applications.* Saint Paul, MN: EMC Publishing.

Bretton Woods Conference [CD-ROM]. (1996). *Microsoft Encarta '96 Encyclopedia.* Microsoft Corporation.

Calhoun, C., Keller, S., & Light, D. (1997). *Sociology* (7th ed.). New York: McGraw-Hill.

Cockerham, W. (1995). *The global society: An introduction to sociology.* New York: McGraw-Hill.

Foreign trade [CD-ROM]. (1996). *Microsoft Encarta '96 Encyclopedia.* Microsoft Corporation.

General agreement on tariffs and trade [CD-ROM]. (1996). *Microsoft Encarta '96 Encyclopedia.* Microsoft Corporation.

Gottheil, F. (1995). *Principles of economics.* Cincinnati, Ohio: Southwestern College.

International monetary fund [CD-ROM]. (1996). *Microsoft Encarta '96 Encyclopedia.* Microsoft Corporation.

Lenski, G., Nolan, P., & Lenski, J. (1995). *Human societies: An introduction to macrosociology* (7th ed.). New York: McGraw-Hill.

McEachern, W. (1997). *Economics, a contemporary introduction* (7th ed.). Cincinnati, OH: Southwestern College.

Reich, R. (1991). *The work of nations: Preparing for twenty-first century capitalism.* New York: Knopf.

Rourke, J. (1997). *International politics on the world stage* (6th ed). Guilford, CT: Dushkin-McGraw-Hill.

Wallerstein, I. (1977). *Rural economy in modern world-society: Vol. 12, No. 1. Studies in comparative international development.* New Brunswick, NJ: Transaction Periodicals Consortium.

World trade organization [CD-ROM]. (1996). *Microsoft Encarta '96 Encyclopedia.* Microsoft Corporation.

7

ASSESSING GLOBAL AWARENESS

Major Points

- Process or feedback evaluation is important in assessing global understanding, attitudes, and actions.
- It is important to relate assessment procedures to clearly stated educational objectives.
- Paper-and-pencil tests are used to assess knowledge on a subject and to verify hypotheses (in the cognitive domain).
- Assessment in the affective domain seeks to establish the attitudes and positions students hold toward the global environment.
- Students, to form grounded positions on global issues, need to trace logical consequences into alternative solutions.
- Assessment in the participatory domain determines whether students, given necessary background knowledge, can act out their concerns and thus participate in discussions on critical world problems.
- Performance or alternative assessment seeks to evaluate students with means such as informal observations, anecdotal records, student projects, journals, and portfolios.

The philosophy of student assessment has changed drastically in recent years. In the past, reliance was placed on paper-and-pencil tests in the spirit of "summative" or "terminal" evaluation. Students were generally judged on what they knew, mostly through questions testing memory. Students passed or failed based on their performance on the test. Students were rarely given a second chance. The new assessment philosophy views student evaluation as an ongoing process; this goal of providing reliable feedback to both students and their teacher helps students know how well they are doing and helps teachers find out how effective they are in delivering instruction (Stiggins, 1994). Under the new philosophy, a variety of assessment procedures are used besides paper-and-pencil tests, including items such as interviews, diaries, journals, self-administered questionnaires, oral presentations, and projects. Informal or authentic assessment of student progress over time is obtained with multiple procedures that can be presented in a portfolio (Kauchak & Eggen, 1998).

The authors of this book are committed to the new philosophy of assessment that relies on process or feedback evaluation to obtain information on student and teacher progress. The key goals of this type of evaluation are to establish how well instruction helps students understand and reflect upon critical issues facing the global community and to develop a predisposition to be part of the emerging global network. The ultimate goal of evaluation is to determine whether instruction generates understanding, interest, and a global consciousness among students and their teachers. A result of this may be the prompting of students to become active in solving world problems.

Chapter 2, which dealt with global education inquiry strategies, presented a table of specifications that can be used by teachers to develop assessment programs in the three target domains—cognitive, affective, and participatory. Sample assessment procedures and test items will be presented for each of the domains.

THE COGNITIVE DOMAIN

In this domain, the essential instructional goal is to assess whether instruction fosters critical or reflective thinking of world issues or problems. The result here is the ability to understand how world problems develop and the consequences of having these problems unresolved. We begin with sample paper-and-pencil instruments seeking to measure the higher mental processes. Using the table of specifications on pages 42–43, zero in on "2.1 Political World Subsystem" (the substantive dimension) and A–K (the skill dimension).

A sample measurable objective emerging from the intersection of C and 2.1 can be stated as, "Given a springboard from a newspaper, students should be able to identify a problem relative to the political world system. A test seeking to measure the objective is presented below."

To the student: Please read the newspaper editorial and answer the questions that follow.

Netanyahu Policy on Settlements Ill Advised, Undermines Peace Talks*

President Clinton's frustration with the policies of Israeli Prime Minister Benjamin Netanyahu finally emerged on Monday. In his sharpest public criticism of Netanyahu, Clinton bluntly said the Israeli government's planned expansion of Jewish settlements on the West Bank was a hindrance to peace.

Responding brusquely, Netanyahu's chief spokesman David Bar-Illan said Washington, not Israel, has to change its position. Inexplicably, Bar-Illan also claimed U.S.–Israeli relations were as good as ever.

Of course, that's preposterous. An annoyed Clinton is beginning to sound like his Republican predecessor, George Bush, who also had to deal with a recalcitrant Likud government intent on expanding West Bank settlements.

Because of the expansion, Bush withheld $10 billion in loan guarantees until after Likud's Yitzhak Shamir lost the June 1992 Israeli election to Yitzhak Rabin. After Clinton won the U.S. election later that year, he was able to work cooperatively with Rabin and Shimon Peres.

That cooperation ended abruptly after Netanyahu came to power this year, and the working relationship between Washington and Jerusalem has been prickly, despite attempts to paper over differences. Now Clinton, disturbed by Netanyahu's encouragement of more Jewish settlers through financial subsidies and tax breaks, has broken the strained politeness with a straightforward comment at a news conference.

*Netenyahu policy on settlements ill advised, undermines peace talks. (1996, December 12). *Sun-Sentinel*, p. 26A. Reprinted with permission from the *Sun-Sentinel*, Fort Lauderdale, Florida.

Clinton's statement obviously had been thought out ahead of time: Settlements were to be part of the final negotiation between Israel and the Palestine Liberation Organization—both sides had so agreed—and anything that "pre-empts the outcome" of those talks "cannot be helpful in making peace."

Asked whether the settlement posed a hindrance to peace, Clinton answered with one crisp word: "Absolutely."

This is the same thorny issue that has hampered Middle East peace negotiations for three decades. The word "settlements" leaves a misperception of what the Jewish communities in Gaza and the West Bank actually are; they're not trailers or tents, but large clusters of solidly built modern houses surrounded by security fences.

Already, the existence of 120,000 Jewish settlers on the West Bank among 1 million Palestinians means any final settlement will result in an irregular checkerboard of Jewish outposts sprinkled through a Palestinian "state." As is it's recipe for war. Adding more settlers makes hostilities more likely, now or later.

Clinton is doing what he can to stave off the total collapse of the peace accords, but it's hard to be anything but pessimistic. If the Palestinians and Israelis are serious about peace, they first have to reach agreement on Israeli withdrawal from Hebron—and eventually an accord on the settlements, without Netanyahu making it worse by expanding them now.

At this holiday season in the tense Holy Land, it's hard to summon up a spirit of peace on Earth, or of goodwill toward one another. Clinton is trying, and for that he should be thanked by both sides.

Identifying a Problem

What is the specific problem as stated in the article? Please circle the appropriate item.

1. President Clinton made a loaded statement.
2. Israel is reluctant to withdraw from Hebron.
*3. The policy of promoting additional Jewish settlements in what were considered to be Palestinian lands is causing trouble for the region's future.
4. East and West are perennially involved in confrontation.

Forming a Hypothesis

What is a plausible hypothesis resulting from the editorial?

1. If President Clinton continues making statements antagonizing Israeli officials, then a world conflict will result.
2. If settlements are secured by fences, then conflict will ensue.
*3. If small settlements of one group of people are created in the midst of a larger group of people with a significantly different cultural heritage, then conflict will develop.
4. Settlements are always a hindrance to peace.

Note: If you believe that none of the hypotheses are used in the editorial, develop your own hypothesis.

Exploring Consequences

According to the editorial, which one of the following would create serious conflict?

1. Clinton's statements
2. Netanyahu's statements
*3. Actual settlements in Arab territories
4. Statements by Arab leaders

Collecting Relevant Data

What type of data would be most useful in testing your hypothesis on the effects of settlements in hostile territories?

1. Statements by the authorities
2. Opinions of world leaders
*3. Results from similar cases
4. Statements by various textbook authors

Making a Generalization and Applying It

1. You have read the editorial concerning the effects of new settlements in hostile lands. Is it likely that the editorial is biased? What would you need to have to validate the evidence presented? Is it possible to generalize the effects described in the article? What would be a defensible generalization, given your

critical review of the article in question and the additional data
you have collected?

2. Now that you have formed a generalization that explains, in part,
   the source of conflict among groups of people with significant
   cultural differences, try to find other cases for which the generalization is applicable. Describe each case clearly and point out
   how the generalization you have formed is applicable. Evaluation criteria of your response include (1) collection of adequate
   relevant data, (2) specificity of answers, (3) Creativity, (4) Clarity
   of expression, and (5) analytical skills used.

All of the sample assessment questions used with the article primarily emphasize the cognitive aspects of teaching and learning global education. The sample items deal with the global dimension in
two different ways. First, the controversy over settlements constitutes
a global concern, because the peace in the Middle East that was obtained through the hard work of a number of countries and international agencies can be compromised if the settlements continue. In
one way or another (e.g., by stoppages of fuel oil transport, by the
UN forcing engagement, or by the Arab world choosing sides and de-
claring war), the whole world would be affected. Second, the global
dimension is introduced from the procedural viewpoint as well, because the hypotheses and generalizations that are formed by students
and teachers apply to all similar cases worldwide. Conflicts during
the 1990s in Cyprus, the former Yugoslavia, and central Africa are
just a few examples for which the main source of conflict was the
inability of groups with different cultural heritages to accommodate
and live peacefully with others. Thus, the whole process of forming
hypotheses to explain certain events and of testing the hypotheses,
resulting in defensible conclusions and generalizations about the
events, has a universal or global character. Simply stated, students
learn to generalize about human behavior and, in that sense, they
operate as social scientists in the quest to explain social phenomena
in their environment. The basic operating assumption is that there
is uniformity in human behavior, historically and temporally.

Another example of cognitive assessment that deals with global
issues is one relating to the integration of quantitative data as presented in charts and tables. Figure 7.1, for instance, provides data
on education and earnings from employment in 19 countries, the

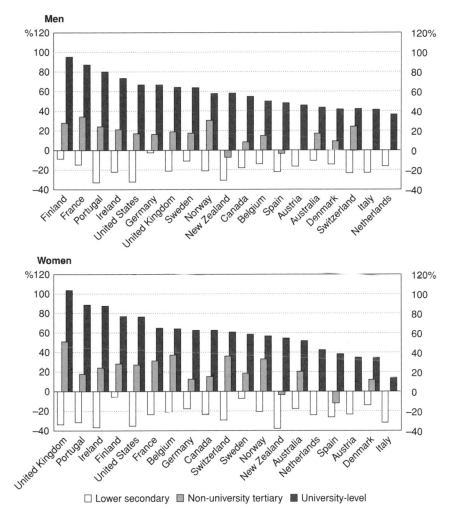

FIGURE 7.1   Education and Earnings from Employment

Mean annual earnings of persons 25 to 64 years of age by level of educational attainment and gender relative to mean annual earnings at the upper secondary level

From Organization for Economic Cooperation and Development (OECD). (1996). *Education at a glance: OECD indicators*. Paris, France: OECD Center for Educational Research and Innovation. Reprinted by permission of OECD.

members of the Organization for Economic Cooperation and Development (OECD). One can construct objective questions that correspond to the letters of the objectives in the cognitive domain ("2.3 Social World Subsystem," A–K) on the tables of specifications in Chapter 2. Examples of such questions include the following:

A. What is the difference, if any, between earnings of university degree holders in Finland and in the Netherlands? Between men and women?

B. What linkage exists between education and employment, if any?

C. Is there a discrepancy in earnings among those completing different levels of education?

D. How does educational attainment affect income?

E. What relational statements are appropriate to explain the differences between levels of educational attainment and income from gainful employment? Are there differences based on gender?

F. What are some of the social consequences of the differential incomes of people?

G. Where would you look and what additional data would you need to explore further the hypothesis on the relation between education and income?

H. Under what categories would you collect your data and how would you analyze the data?

I. If you have a new idea of how to increase the earnings of people your age, how would you go about testing it out?

J. What is your conclusion on how level of educational attainment affects earnings from gainful employment? How does gender affect earnings, other factors being equal?

K. Would your conclusions or generalizations apply to the situations in countries other than OECD members? How would you go about finding out?

It is clear from these questions that the overall focus of the lesson centers on the idea that the more education one has, the more income one is likely to have. This is certainly substantiated by the data from all 19 countries presented in Figure 7.1. There are also obvious earning differences between the different countries as well as between men and women. One can follow another line of questioning beginning with these differences and then hypothesizing about the special factors generating these differences. One could also look at data on education and unemployment, especially among youths. During this process, however, one important point should be kept in mind—the importance of keeping a global framework in the investigation. Is the experience of the OECD countries applicable to the entire world? Do the hypotheses and generalizations apply equally to the developed as well as the developing world? How does this phenomenon affect oneself as well as family and friends? Should certain action be taken?

Needless to say, both exercises—the one based on the editorial and the one on education and earnings—lend themselves well to questions of affect, and global, social participation. Questions of equity and fairness are certainly in order for both exercises. Participatory questions prompting action can also be raised in both instances. Instruction in all three domains focuses on global topics, and the issues contribute to the development of a global consciousness in students. As they engage in relevant inquiry, students begin to realize that they are members of the global village and that anything happening in the most remote part of the world directly or indirectly affects them and other members of their local community.

THE AFFECTIVE DOMAIN

This domain deals with appreciation, attitudes, and values. We develop affinities toward certain things, institutions, and people as well as positive, negative, and neutral orientations toward certain practices in our environment. We take positions for or against certain policies. We openly express our preferences, while often preferences are merely implicit in our actions. Within a global perspective we show interest on global topics and issues; we take stands on such issues; and we try to defend these stands on warranted and communicable grounds. We also develop sensitivities toward our fellow global citizens, trying to understand them and empathize with them. At the highest level in the affective domain, we internalize the value of being a global citizen and understand how the global system operates.

Exercises and assessment items in the affective domain do not lend themselves to "objective" procedures whereby the reliability of a statement can be ascertained. Values that people hold cannot be considered true or false. Rather, value statements and expressions of preferences are as good as the grounds that support them. The following are key questions: Are the positions taken by students on a certain global issue defensible? Are the grounds on which their positions rest communicable? Are the students being understood by all concerned? It is in this spirit that the exercise based on the article entitled, "Blending of Cultures Created Friction in Tolerant Vancouver," is offered. The questions correspond to letters of the objectives in the table of specifications, ("2.3 Social World Subsystems," and U–GG) in Chapter 2.

To the student: Please read the article "Tensions Rise in Tolerant Vancouver" by Howard Schneider (1996) and answer the questions that follow. Explain your answers in detail and write at least one paragraph.

*Tensions Rise in Tolerant Vancouver**

Vancouver, B. C.—Among the first things Thomas Tam tells this city's new arrivals from Hong Kong, Taiwan and elsewhere in Asia is advice about shifting gears: Keep your voice down in public, and whenever possible, speak English.

It might sound like jarring counsel in a continent where individual rights are paramount, and particularly in Canada, which is officially bilingual and multicultural. Despite immigration policies constructed around the premise of tolerance, Tam said that Canada remains a place where Anglo–Canadian sensitivities are easily riled.

Even in Vancouver, a place generally considered easygoing, the cultures do not always blend easily, said Tam, administrator of a Chinese social services group. Asian immigration, particularly from Hong Kong as it prepares for next year's [1997] takeover by China, has changed the face of Vancouver during the past two decades. In doing so, it also has tested the city's ability to meet Canada's ideal of society as a mosaic of cultures.

Generally, "the tolerance level is high," Tam said, but "some people have the concept of the host and the guest: 'You come to my place, you speak my language'" and otherwise adapt to the surroundings.

"We tell the new immigrants, first, the voice. [In] Hong Kong and Taiwan, they speak loud. It is very noisy and crowded. ...They forget Canada is a quieter place," Tam said. "And we want them to use English when Canadian people are around."

It is a paradox in the fabric of life here: The tolerance level is indeed high, so high that Vancouver, on Canada's Pacific coast, is now a city where a majority of families cite languages other than English as the one they use at home. Yet where the cultures intersect—at the schools and in the neighborhoods—there has been tension as new and old residents try to build a relationship and clash over differences as subtle as the size of an entrance.

In West Vancouver, long-established and sometimes modest neighborhoods quickly changed character as affluent Asian immigrants moved in and put up what came to be dubbed the "monster houses." With two-story entrances and double doors—and built as close to property lines as possible—the structures gave a seesaw character to some blocks as they tower over their smaller neighbors.

"People were coming and tearing down a nice house and building a new one that wasn't fitting in," said Jack Benfield, a resident of the city's Shaugnassy neighborhood and one of the activists involved in developing new zoning restrictions.

The latest debate concerns trees. The newcomers clear-cut their lots and leave once leafy downtown neighborhoods bare, prompting proposals in the city council for limits on changes that homeowners may make to their property.

"When you talk about issues like preserving trees, they are proxy issues," said Victor Wong, president of the Vancouver Association of Chinese Canadians. "It is more about the type of person you want in your neighborhood, the type of kid you want for your child's classmate. It is a much bigger issue."

The Asian presence is nothing new in British Columbia. Wong said there has been an established Chinese community in the province since the mid-1800s, and about 20 percent of Vancouverites are not ethnic Chinese.

But the wave of new arrivals in the past decade from Hong Kong, Taiwan and elsewhere, Wong said, created a new "business class" of Asian Vancouverites who, while investing billions of dollars and buoying the providence's economy, also began changing the nature of traditionally white neighborhoods in and around Vancouver.

Since tensions began rising in the 1980s, building regulations have become increasingly restrictive. First, laws were passed ordering that smaller houses be built and restricting the size of second stories. The rules were approved that awarded property owners the right to use more space if their designs were first reviewed by the city for consistency with other homes in the neighborhood.

Finally, neighborhoods were given the option of adopting their own building restrictions, down to details such as the size of the entrance or the color of the roof. Hanson Lay, executive producer for a local multilingual radio station, said some of the zoning restrictions are culturally insulting, such as the rule that prohibits red roofs. For Chinese, red is the traditional color for happiness.

"It is a very subtle racism manifestation," he said. "Why not a purple roof after you pay $2 million?"

U. In your own words, what is the issue at stake?

V. What is your own position on the issue?

W. On what evidence and reasons is your position based?

X. What are your feelings toward the newly arrived immigrants in Vancouver? What are your feelings toward the Anglo–Canadians?

Y. Is it fair to require all immigrants to speak English? Is it fair to have to compromise your own customs and habits to accommodate newly arrived immigrants?

Z. Should a city that professes to be a "mosaic of cultures" promote policies that do not provide equitable opportunities for all ethnic groups to prosper and advance?

AA. Was the purpose of the new laws just to enact rules and regulations that promote the interests of one group of people over another?

BB. If you were an arbitrator trying to judge whether the new city policies were discriminatory, what would you do to maintain your objectivity?

CC. Would you be interested in pursuing the study of the issue at stake further by interviewing city officials? Interviewing members of each ethnic group? Checking other references in the library? Writing an editorial on the issue in your school paper?

DD. Do you trust the city officials to do the right thing?

Describe which of the following groups you trust to do the right thing: new arrivals from Asia, Anglo–Canadians, U.S. citizens, or "global citizens"?

EE. If you were a resident of Vancouver, would you feel compelled to change the prevailing tense situation between the ethnic groups?

FF. If you were a U.S. citizen in Vancouver and lived there for a long time, would you feel like a member of the society or still feel like a foreigner?

GG. What other examples in the world demonstrate similarities to the Vancouver case? Explain in detail.

This exercise clearly relates to issues that have global ramifications. The substance of the issue concerns the question of whether groups of people with different cultural backgrounds can coexist peacefully. The case of Vancouver, as described in the article, represents a microcosm of the globe where all cultural groups meet and interact with each other. If such interactions are marked by excessive ethnocentrism, then a number of hostile acts as described in the article can follow. If, on the other hand, people of different ethnic and cultural backgrounds begin to understand and empathize with each other, then tranquillity can ensue and a global consciousness can prevail that makes each member of the community feel and behave like a global citizen. A global citizen is a citizen who is characterized by an attitude of openness toward all others, irrespective of their gender, race, ethnicity, age, religion, and language. This does not mean that they give up their own beliefs and values and do not respect their own culture. It simply means that they understand and appreciate other cultures and are tolerant of the differences that exist. Thus, the global perspective prevails over nationalistic, ethnocentric, and provincial views. While there are no right and wrong answers to the questions in the exercise, students and their teachers can easily detect whether instruction has assisted even in a limited way to develop a global consciousness among students.

Procedurally speaking, students are asked to reveal their own feelings on the issue and to clarify them under a rigorous examination in the open forum of ideas. They learn to form positions on global problems and how to apply criteria of fairness, equity, and justice in solving these problems. It is understood that the affective skills they learn in the classroom can be generalized to other global problems and issues.

THE PARTICIPATORY DOMAIN

This domain deals with social and political action, an objective that is rarely implemented in schools. The other domains test for student ability to explain the world and to take positions on issues dealing with the world's problems; however, thinking about and developing certain orientations toward the world do not change the world. To bring about change, one needs to participate actively in the process. One needs to learn the organizational skills to function as a change agent.

In the table of specifications in Chapter 2, the participatory skills are listed on the vertical column (L–T). Assuming these skills are promoted in daily lessons, their assessment is required along with the assessment of the skills in the two domains previously examined. The content of the illustrative exercises could be applied here to assess the skills of participation. For example, students could be asked to develop plans of participation and then actually participate in changing certain world situations that they consider unfair. Such situations have been presented in the articles on new Jewish settlements in Palestine and cultural conflicts in Vancouver and by examining the OECD chart on education and earnings. As discussed in the chapter on instructional methodology, before students can engage in participatory acts they need to develop a high sense of global political and social efficacy—a sense that they understand how the world system operates and that they feel confident in being able to change it. If students and their teachers do not reach the state of feeling competent to bring about change in the global environment, meaningful participatory acts are not likely to take place.

The following article, "Christian Suffering on the Rise," by Jeff Jacoby in the *Boston Globe* detailing examples of worldwide religious persecution is a springboard for discussion. The students are asked to read the article and answer the participatory questions that follow. The questions correspond to letters of the objectives in the table of specifications ("2.3 Social World Subsystems" and L–T) in Chapter 2.

To the student: Please read the article on religious persecution and answer the questions that follow.

Christian Suffering on the Rise*

"Fear not: for behold, I bring you good tidings of great joy." Every Christian knows what the angel said to those shepherds 20 centuries ago as a baby lay sleeping in a Bethlehem manger. Here in America, where the most powerful community of Christians in history dwells in peace and prosperity, the story of Jesus has indeed proved a fount of good tidings and great joy. "Fear not," the angel, said. But in this right and blessed place Christians need not fear. Their freedom to worship is unchallenged; their religious liberty is enshrined in law.

But for millions of Christians in other lands, fear is ever present. Never before—never before—have so many believers in Jesus been persecuted for their faith. "Christians are the chief victims of…religious persecution around the world today," writes Nina Shea of Freedom House, the renowned human rights organization. "In many countries they suffer not just discrimination or bigotry but torture, imprisonment, and the ultimate test of faith, martyrdom."

Shea is the author of *In the Lion's Den*, one of two forthcoming books documenting the global plague of anti-Christian persecution. The other is *Their Blood Cries Out* by Paul Marshall, a senior academic at the Institute for Christian Studies in Toronto.

*Jacoby, J. (1996, December 9). Christian suffering on the rise. *The Boston Globe*, p. A15. Reprinted courtesy of the *Boston Globe*.

Both will come as jolting reality checks to anyone who imagines that violence against Christians ended with the Roman Empire. It is true that over the span of Western history, Christians have been guilty of brutal atrocities. From the Crusades to the Inquisition to the blood libels of Czarist Russia, horrifying evil has been committed in Jesus' name. But today in the East, it is Christians who are hunted and martyred. Whenever militant Islam has taken hold and wherever Communist dictators still rule, Christians are in desperate danger.

The testimony with which Shea and Marshall have filled their books is heart stopping.

Sudan, the Nuba Mountains: "These mountains, which have had a Christian population since the 6th century, are littered with mass graves...Nuba women are systematically raped by Arab soldiers in order to produce non-Nuba offspring. There have been reports, including from Catholic bishops, of crucifixions of Christians by the army." Muslim troops from northern Sudan have sold tens of thousands of Christian children and women from the south into slavery. Many have been branded or mutilated to prevent escape; many more have been tortured, brainwashed or starved until they converted to Islam.

China, Shaanxi Province: "The officers stripped three brethren naked from the waist and forced the women to stand with them...The three men were beaten until they were totally covered with blood and had gaping wounds and injuries all over their bodies. As if such violent beatings weren't enough, the officer then hung them up and began to hit them with rods on their backs. They did this until the three men were unconscious and barely breathing." The victims were Protestants. Their crime was communicating with foreigners.

Pakistan: "The Muslim population of Khan Jajja (was) incited in May 1994 by the local Muslim cleric to drive 60 Christian families of the region from the 'land of the pure' and to demolish their church. The Christian men were beaten and the women were stripped naked...while three girls were kidnapped and raped. These Christians' homes were razed and their possessions looted or destroyed." Pakistan's 1986 blasphemy law makes it a capital crime to insult the Prophet Mohammed "by any imputation, innuendo or insinuation." The law has been used repeatedly to justify a reign of terror against Pakistani Christians.

Nigeria, Kano State: "The leaflet that was mass-distributed to Christians...in 1995 was both ominous and explicit: 'This is to inform you that for your interest and life security, you are seriously advised to pack out of Kano metropolis with immediate effect; otherwise your life will be in danger.... No authority can protect you from whatever calamity may befall you if you fail to comply.' The...leaflet, written by the Islamist group Ja'amatu Tajudidi Islamiya, was delivered in the wake of a new round of Muslim–Christian violence in Kano that had left one Protestant pastor dead and several Christian churches burned to the ground."

Earlier this year the Armed Islamic Group in Algeria slit the throats of seven Trappist monks. Police in China's Zhejiang Province demolished 15,000 Christian temples and tombs. A U.S. citizen visiting her native village in Vietnam was arrested for giving Bible tapes and pens adorned with crosses. Three Coptic Christian villages in Egypt's Nile Delta were torched by Muslim mobs in February. Seven foreigners were imprisoned and beaten in Saudi Arabia for holding a private worship service last Christmas.

This has been a century of unmatched Christian martyrdom. It began with the mass murder of Christians in Armenia; it is ending with the mass murder of Christians in Sudan. Then as now, the world looked away, even as it looked away during the most unspeakable mass murder of all, the Holocaust.

Will we look away again? "Fear not," the angel said. Yet never before have so many Christians had reason to fear. Which means that never before have Christians in America, whose lives brim with good tidings of great joy, been called more urgently to pray for, and cry out for, their embattled brethren.

    L. Given the article you have read, have you recently observed similar incidents of religious persecution in your community, in your school, in your country, and/or in the world?

    M. Do you support Jacoby's view that "for Christians in other lands, fear is ever-present"? Can you find examples other than those given by the author in which non-Christians have been persecuted as well? Explain in detail.

N. If your observations have confirmed that there is religious persecution in your school, in your community, in your country, or in the world, what do you propose to do? What action plan do you have in mind? Detail the main elements of your proposal.

O. Once you have a well-constructed proposal for action, how would you go about mobilizing support? Depending on the level in which you are operating (local, state, national, global), give examples of informal groups, agencies, associations, or world organizations you would contact to gain support for your proposal.

P. Assuming you have brought together a group of people (your fellow students and school teachers, your family, community members), how would you organize them in order to carry our your plan of action? In other words, how would you distribute the tasks among your group members so that the organizational goals can be attained?

Q. What do you anticipate to be your gain or loss as you engage in this type of action to change an unfair policy or practice?

R. Assuming you have reached the key decision makers, what bargaining conditions (conditions that would not damage your cause) can you draw?

S. Once your action has brought about some tangible results, what kind of policy or rule could you create so that religious persecution would not reoccur among the groups of people you were concerned about?

T. How can you bring the policy to a vote by all concerned? Would you require a simple majority to confirm this rule?

As illustrated by these questions, the assessment seeks to establish whether students, as a result of instruction, know how to go about changing an unfair rule or policy. It should be noted, however, that if the unfair practice is observed outside one's immediate community, there might be reluctance to engage in participatory acts. In such a case, the teacher should promote a classroom environment in which students feel strongly that they can influence the global system. To strengthen their global efficacy, students can learn such things as how to contact an international agency, how to access the international media, and how to approach people anywhere in the world to gain support for their views and positions. Students in the global classroom should develop the feeling that they are an inextricable part of the world and, as such, they have the right and responsibility to act out their worldviews.

ALTERNATIVE ASSESSMENT

So far we have focused on paper-and-pencil tests that provide information to the teachers and students on how well they are doing in their quest to develop a global perspective. In this section we will deal with three forms of alternative assessment: informal observations, performance assessment, and portfolios (Airasian, 1994).

Informal observations constitute the majority of assessment occurrences in the classroom. When a student asks a question of another student, or when a teacher asks questions of a student, an informal observation assessment is beginning to take place. The discussion that follows these questions provides the basis of informal observation and assessment.

The questions asked in class usually determine the nature of the answer. If the question asks for information, a recall type of answer follows. In our view, all classroom participants should stress reflective type questions. As per Bloom's taxonomy, the following questions are illustrations of what can be asked to elicit lower or higher level thinking among classroom participants on the topic of the global environment. (Kauchak & Eggen, 1998).

- What did the Montreal Protocol of 1989 have to say about the quest for ozone layer protection? (lower level question)
- What specific problems for humans are caused by ozone depletion, and how can they be prevented? (higher level question)

- Which countries in the world have the highest incidence of acid rain? (lower level question)
- Is there a relationship between acid rain and deforestation? (higher level question)

- What are the countries with the highest and lowest human populations? (lower level question)
- What are the connections, if any, between rapid population growth and environmental pollution? Explain. (higher level question)

Classroom participants, including teachers, can draw various inferences about the level of a person's performance in response to these questions. Thus, informal observation assessments are constantly made during the class period. Naturally, some of these observations are incomplete, biased, and easily forgotten. To reduce the incidence of distorted or unreliable assessment through observations, teachers often use an "anecdotal record." Such a record is usually a short written statement of a student's behavior during a given period. The anecdotal record would contain essential information about the student and, if needed, a recommendation by the teacher for improvement. Here is an example:

Anecdotal Record: Interested Student

Date: December 2, 1999

Student's Name: John Doe

Teacher's Name: Mr. McCarthey

Behavior: John was able to identify several relationships between rapid population growth and the deterioration of the world's ecosystem.

Inference: John is interested in discussions of global affairs and can perform at the higher levels of thinking.

Recommendation: He should be continuously provided with challenging problems facing the world. Additional activities including readings should be made available to him.

This example of an anecdotal record refers to a student who exhibits interest in global studies. For a student who does not, the record might show the following:

Anecdotal Record: Uninterested Student

<u>Date:</u>	December 2, 1999
<u>Student's Name:</u>	Art Hinkle
<u>Teacher's Name:</u>	Mr. McCarthey
<u>Behavior:</u>	Art acts withdrawn most of the time in class discussions of global environmental issues. He does not seem to be interested in the subject. Attempts to draw him into the discussion have failed.
<u>Inference:</u>	The subject matter presented in class does not challenge Art. He seems to be interested in other things, sports being one of them.
<u>Recommendation:</u>	Prepare lessons that address sports and athletics on an international level. Try to involve Art in activities related to this topic.

Checklists and rating scales can also be used for informal assessment. They are actually used to assess authentic performance, which is the extent to which students go beyond the content of the topic studied; it demonstrates the student's ability to apply a concept, a skill, or a policy statement to a new situation. The assessment instrument used can measure the process or the product of student effort. An example of a checklist used by a teacher to record performance is as follows:

Checklist

Student's Name_____   Date:_____

_____1. Student knows how to collect relevant data to support hypotheses on the relationship between human activities and the preservation of the environment (process skill).

_____2. Student forms a theory that explains why world organizations are instrumental in promoting acceptance of and respect for human rights. (product skill)

_____3. Student knows how to interpret statistical tables, charts, and graphs on such topics as environmental pollution, population change, and distribution of educational services worldwide. (process skill)

_____4. Student identifies areas in the world where deforestation is most acute and designs plans to ease the difficulty. (product skill)

_____5. Student organizes a group of students and their parents to send a petition to the Secretary General of the United Nations to stop or curtail governments in specific countries from discriminating against certain groups of people because of their religious beliefs. (process skill)

_____6. Student demonstrates strong interest in discussing political issues that have worldwide implications. (affect, attitude)

_____7. Student expresses empathy for people suffering from malnutrition in certain areas of the world. (affect, attitude)

_____8. Student writes a letter to the World Health Organization asking that measures be taken to prevent farmers in the developing world from being poisoned from pesticides. (affect, attitude)

The items checked by the teacher indicate that the student in question was observed applying that particular skill. Rating scales can also be developed using the same or similar items. The scale can range from one to five, with five being the highest performance level. These numbers in the scale can then be identified with a range of words from "never" to "always." It should be noted that all informal measures of performance should be related to instructional objectives, samples of which emerge from the intersection of behaviors or skills and substantive concepts or experiences (as presented in the table of specifications in Chapter 2).

Student portfolios are also used in assessing student progress over time. A portfolio, like an artist's portfolio, is supposed to include examples of what the student is capable of doing (Farr & Tone, 1994). Corrected paper-and-pencil tests and quizzes may be part of the portfolio but, in addition, projects, art, other creative work, and observation reports form a good portion of each portfolio. The teacher, who has provided some initial guidelines in setting up the portfolio, can observe progress over time when meeting with each student to review the portfolio. The content of the portfolios should always relate to the instructional objectives that the class works to attain.

Student projects containing both product and process skills can be included in portfolios. On the subject of world ecological problems, the following ideas may serve as initial springboards to engage students in project development:

- relationships between a rapidly increasing world population and environmental pollution; for instance, water pollution, thermal pollution, air pollution, or radioactive waste
- past, present, and needed future initiatives for ozone layer protection
- causes of deforestation and what each individual or group can do to prevent the rapid disappearance of forests
- the effects of different types of mining on the environment
- the effects of the uneven distribution of people in the world

These ideas can be simplified so that even students at the elementary school level can understand them and develop a project around them. Guidelines for carrying out projects, such as how to form hypotheses and how to go about testing them, should be available to students of all ages. As each project develops step-by-step, progress reports are placed in the portfolio. Thus, both students and teacher have a record of performance over time.

More difficult, of course, is to record results from actual participation in global affairs. While a copy of a letter to a UN representative may be placed in the portfolio, actual conversations—such as telephone calls to decision makers—are difficult to record. It is possible, however, to encourage students who participate in community or, through representatives, in the world community to keep a log of their activities so that their efforts in this domain can be recognized and assessed. A student participatory log or journal may look like the following example:

Journal of Activity: Nancy Hawthorn

8/25/98   Called UN Secretariat in New York to get information about and address of the World Health Organization.

8/31/98   Wrote letter to WHO Secretary to ask what the agency is doing to prevent farmers in developing areas from dying from the use of pesticides.

9/10/98   Interviewed local Congresswoman asking what the U.S. Congress can do to resolve the problem.

9/12/98   Received letter from WHO with information on ongo-
           ing projects.
9/23/98   Met with Congresswoman's assistant to review letter
           and information from WHO.
9/25/98   Sent group letter to all elected state representatives in
           Washington D.C. and to the President asking that they
           financially support WHO, earmarking funds in support
           of farmers in the designated high mortality lands.

This log, kept by a student, suggests a way in which participatory
activity can be recorded and assessed. A well-organized portfolio
with an appropriately recorded list of events and with other topic-
related materials can provide a much better base to make an assessment decision than any single instrument.

SUMMARY

This chapter dealt with various means of classroom assessment,
focusing on the development of global understanding and consciousness through the application of cognitive, affective, and participatory skills to global issues. Bloom's notion of a conceptual map
to guide the formation of educational objectives was used as a
framework, with the use of a table of specifications focusing on global affairs. The sample assessment measures presented in the chapter
were developed in the spirit of formative or feedback evaluation
rather than summative or formal evaluation.

The main objective in the cognitive domain is to encourage students to develop and test hypotheses that seek to explain how the
global system and its subsystems operate. In accomplishing this objective, students learn how to tap relevant sources in the library or
through the Internet. They also learn how to sift data and use only
the data that relate to their hypotheses. Finally, they learn how to
arrive at a conclusion about the state of the world that is based on
reliable evidence and has wide applicability. The assessment materials presented here help to establish whether these skills have been
properly acquired.

The key objective in the affective domain is to encourage students to develop warranted positions on global issues. For example,
abrupt population changes, environmental pollution, global drug

trafficking, the use of violent means to solve disputes between sovereign states, and the unrestricted use of the open seas are issues of global importance. Students also learn how to apply normative criteria (e.g., fairness, justice, and equality) to world situations in order to maintain a system that promotes human survival. Assessment procedures emphasize appreciations, attitudes, and values that classroom participants hold in their quest to resolve global issues that inescapably have local and personal ramifications.

Using participatory skills, students seek to carry out decisions reached through the application of cognitive and affective skills. The assessment in this area seeks to find out how well students have become active in trying to influence decisions that have worldwide implications. These assessments actually establish how well students go about organizing themselves in dealing with local, state, national, or world decision makers. Have their organizational efforts brought results? Have certain policies been changed because of student action? If not, what else can be done to bring about desirable changes?

The assessment of student and teacher growth need not rely on paper-and-pencil tests only. Informal assessment procedures can also be used as well. Informal observations, anecdotal records, checklists, rating scales, and portfolios are means of assessment, especially the assessment of complex types of operations such as the operations described in the text. Informal assessment measures give teachers and their students a better index of their capabilities than formal assessment measures. These informal measures also allow all concerned to observe changes of performance over a period of time: a six-week period, a semester, or an academic year.

The main goal of assessment in the field of global studies is to measure the extent to which globalization, both in substance and in process, is understood and internalized by the classroom participants. If that goal is reached, then the most important instructional purpose will have been achieved.

QUESTIONS FOR REFLECTION

1. Do you agree or disagree with the authors' position that the main purpose of student assessment is to identify strengths and weaknesses in the instructional process and to establish areas where additional work is needed (feedback or process evaluation)? Justify your position.

2. After selecting the appropriate educational objectives from the table of specifications, find an editorial reporting on an issue with global implications from a current edition of a newspaper. Develop a paper-and-pencil test for the editorial following the examples presented in this chapter and assessing students in the cognitive domain.

3. After you have completed the test, try it out with your class and make the appropriate changes. Administer the test again to establish its face validity—whether it measures what it intends to measure.

4. Given the objectives you have identified for your lesson on global issues, select a springboard for your lesson (an article, a picture, a cartoon, a chart, a graph, a table, or a video) and develop a set of assessment terms in the affective domain. As in the example in the chapter, through these items test the students' ability to articulate a position on a global issue and follow it with an action proposal.

5. Given the objectives you selected for your lesson in response to question 5, develop a set of items that would give you and your students a record of their ability, and yours, to operate effectively in the participatory domain. Can they act out their assigned positions? Will their actions bring about change? How will they mobilize support? These are some of the questions that need to be answered in this domain.

6. What is actually meant by "authentic assessment"? Does this type of assessment provide a better picture of student potential than the traditional paper-and-pencil tests and standardized instruments? What is your position on this issue?

7. Given the objectives for your lesson on a global issue, develop and field-test the following alternative assessment procedures:

   - student diaries
   - projects
   - journals
   - anecdotal records
   - observations
   - personal communications
   - portfolios

   Which ones provide the most reliable assessment information? Explain.

8. Many assessment questions result in some type of essay responses from students. When you read these essays, what criteria would you use in evaluating them? Explain why.

REFERENCES

Airasian, P. (1994). *Classroom assessment* (2nd ed.). New York: McGraw-Hill.

Farr, R., & Tone, B. (1994). *Portfolio performance assessment.* Fort Worth, TX: Harcourt Brace.

Jacoby, J. (1996, December 9). Christian suffering on the rise. *The Boston Globe,* p. A15.

Kauchak, D., & Eggen, P. (1998). *Learning and teaching: Research based methods* (3rd ed.). Boston: Allyn & Bacon.

Netanyahu policy on settlements ill advised, undermines peace talks. (1996, December 12). *Sun-Sentinel,* p. A26.

Organization for Economic Cooperation and Development (OECD). (1996). *Education at a glance: OECD indicators.* Paris, France: OECD Center for Educational Research and Innovation.

Schneider, H. (1996, December 16). Tensions rise in tolerant Vancouver. *The Washington Post,* p. A18.

Stiggins, R. (1994). *Student-centered classroom assessment.* New York: Merrill-Macmillan.

8

A NEW ERA FOR
GLOBAL EDUCATION

Major Points

- Implementing global education is important in meeting the promises and challenges of the twenty-first century and the new millennium.

- The purpose of global education must be made clear to students and teachers alike.

- There are different types of pedagogy that are appropriate for global education.

- Criteria must be identified in order to select appropriate global education curricula.

- Instructional strategies need to be consistent with the aims of global education.

- It is important to identify key concepts and issues to trigger thinking in the classroom.

- A variety of assessment procedures can reflect the goals of global education.

With globalization being a worldwide phenomenon, we have entered a new era in providing global education to children enrolled in the nation's schools. There is an increasing realization that nations and people depend on each other for survival. A change in a

Pacific current, such as El Niño, can immediately have wide ramifications in the entire world. Limiting oil production in the Middle East can automatically cause turbulence in the rest of the world. The long lines of cars waiting for gasoline when the flow of oil was disrupted in the 1970s are still remembered on the North American continent as well as in Europe and other parts of the world. The stock price drop of over 10% in the Hong Kong market in 1997 affected all the stock markets of the world. Indeed, it is very difficult to find any major political, economic, social, or ecological event happening in one of the world's regions without instantaneous or long-term implications for the rest of the world. The "splendid isolation" of nations in past centuries is no longer an option for any country in the world.

World interdependence and globalization, are here to stay for at least the near future. Unless citizens of all nations are knowledgeable about activities in the world system, they are going to be limited in their ability to function effectively and adequately perform their rights and responsibilities as citizens. Reliable knowledge and understanding of world affairs is a precondition for individuals and groups to make sound political, economic, and ecological decisions. With an understanding of the world system, individuals begin to develop a consciousness that they are members of the world community and empathetic feelings toward their fellow world citizens. However, cognitive knowledge and understanding of the world and a global consciousness are not enough. Citizens of the twenty-first century need to have the skills as well as the determination to act—to participate, directly or indirectly—on decisions that affect them. As a result of knowledge, understanding, and a propensity to act, citizens develop a cosmopolitan rather than a provincial attitude toward their sociopolitical and economic environment, and they increase their sense of individual efficacy (i.e., they develop the attitude that they are in a position to control their life destiny).

Given that world conditions require citizens to have a global perspective in their daily decisions and activities, what can schools do to facilitate and encourage the acquisition of this perspective? This text has sought to provide a pedagogy that would promote the development of this global perspective in students of all ages. The ideas in this section are offered in the spirit of inquiry and need to be critically examined, discussed, and criticized.

WHAT IS GLOBAL EDUCATION?

We began this text seeking to clarify the meaning of global education; writing that global education is a pedagogy that aims at student learning of global concepts and issues and leads to citizen action. We made a distinction between global education and multicultural education in the sense that global education focuses on world issues and multicultural education emphasizes issues that are indigenous to the country in which students and their teachers live. Both fields, however, share a great deal in common: a humanism that makes all of the earth's occupants have compassion for their fellow citizens—citizens of the local, state, or world communities. They share also the educational values of promoting equity, human rights, and mutual respect. Both fields emphasize instructional strategies that foster an inquisitive spirit among students, encouraging them to make inquiries and critically examine issues in their local and world environments.

This book has also emphasized the distinction between mainstream academic knowledge and transformative knowledge and has indicated how important it is for teachers to introduce and point to the discrepancies existing between the two when interpreting national or world events. For example, students may be asked to compare events leading to the American Revolution as described in U.S. textbooks and British textbooks. Students can also be asked to read about the period of industrial development in the United States and compare the conclusions of U.S. authors with Russian authors writing in the *Great Soviet Encyclopedia*. Which interpretation of a period of U.S. history is accurate? Students, easily determining the obvious contradictions, would, with the prompting of the teacher, seek to find new interpretations (transformative knowledge) of what really happened. In other words, the use of transformative knowledge in the classroom opens up the possibility for students to learn to question myths and inaccuracies conveyed to them through the standard textbooks and through the hidden curriculum.

When new ideas that challenge traditional content enter the classroom, then controversy is created; however, students need to feel that the controversy touches their lives and their well-being. If they do not experience this, the controversy may just be another purely academic discussion over a matter of specialists' concerns.

"No taxation without representation" might have been a rallying slogan during the American Revolution, but it can also be connected with current conditions in many parts of the world. In both the developed and developing world, disadvantaged populations are taxed, but their representation and influence in the political process are either minimal or nonexistent. Is the student studying such an event affected by this social condition? If students are affected, what can they individually or collectively do to alter the situation for the better?

WHAT TYPE OF PEDAGOGY IS APPROPRIATE FOR GLOBAL EDUCATION?

Key elements in any pedagogical scheme for maximizing learning in the classroom include a clear statement of educational objectives, a relevant curriculum, and effective instructional strategies. According to Benjamin Bloom, educational objectives can be placed in separate, logical and psychologically defensible categories. These categories are the cognitive, the affective, and the psychomotor. In this book the authors have added another category, the participatory, and excluded the psychomotor because it is not quite applicable to the field of global education.

Following Bloom's conceptualization, we developed a table of specifications found in Chapter 2 that provides examples of educational objectives for global education. Skills and behaviors combined with concepts and data from various academic fields, such as political science, sociology, economics, history, and geography, are stated as objectives. As explained in this text, skills and behaviors comprise the procedural dimension in the matrix; concepts and data from the various disciplines of knowledge comprise the substantive dimension. Within the substantive dimension we have also included the experiences that all classroom participants bring to the classroom. While the table of specifications we have constructed provides only an example of how the field can be presented, it shows how teachers can procedurally clarify objectives. We do not subscribe to a mechanistic formulation of objectives and their implementation in the classroom; rather, we advocate a general plan that enables the teacher to be systematic in the development of sound goals and objectives and to implement them with relevant curriculum, instructional methods, and assessment procedures.

WHAT TYPE OF CURRICULUM IS NEEDED?

The book began with the assumption that global issues can be taught to students of all ages, starting with kindergarten. Rather than developing a separate course in an already crowded school curriculum, we advanced and demonstrated through example the idea of infusing the standard curriculum with global concepts and issues. Thus, global studies can be infused into all subjects taught in school—social studies, language arts, science, math, home economics, foreign language, physical education, art, and music.

Student interest in world affairs is generated with the introduction of controversial issues. In fact, the type of curriculum proposed here is a series of events or social phenomena that have created controversy in the past and continue to create problems and controversies. While we give some ideas about the global content to be infused into the curriculum, level by level, we also provide information to the reader on global issues we consider to be important: human rights, population, and refugees; the environment, energy, health, and nutrition; and global economics and security. Teachers can extract the concepts and the issues that need to be discussed in their classrooms depending on their educational objectives: Would students with limited English proficiency be interested in discussing issues dealing with refugees and their rights? Would students from a low socioeconomic status be interested in discussing world issues concerning the distribution of wealth? Would students who are transported to schools in overcrowded buses and enter an overcrowded classroom be interested in how other countries have solved this problem? Each chapter provides information on such issues and offer suggestions for activities to engage students.

As stated earlier, teachers are asked to select materials that are controversial (i.e., they are controversial in society and concern the students and their families). Research indicates that when the substance of lessons involves controversial issues and students are engaged in critically analyzing these issues, learning takes place.

In selecting issues to be included in the global curriculum the following criteria can be used (Massialas, 1996):

1. *The criterion of relevance.* Is the issue related to the student's interest, background, and concerns?
2. *The criterion of reflection.* The key concern here is whether the content of the lesson triggers thinking.
3. *The criterion of action.* Does the content prompt students to initiate some type of reasonable action?
4. *The criterion of practicality.* Is the proposed content usable in the sense that the normal tranquillity of the school is not going to be disrupted, for example by irate parents or administrators?
5. *Depth of understanding.* Does the curriculum provide adequate sources so that the student examines the issue from all points of view?

Another important point to be made is that while there is a formal curriculum, there is also a hidden curriculum, or covert curriculum, which has not been taken into account by most educators. The formal curriculum explicitly states what the purposes of schooling should be: to promote academic achievement, good citizenship, and training for gainful employment. The hidden curriculum, on the other hand, more subtly conveys messages and prompts actions that have powerful effects on learning and instruction. For example, hidden messages in textbooks often depict the United States as being the "best country in the world" and other countries as inferior. This message would contradict aims stated in the school's curriculum, which likely states that students should look objectively at the world and each country's strengths and weaknesses. The hidden curriculum enters the classroom through the actions of the teacher as well. If the teacher's view of the world is provincial, global understanding and the development of a global consciousness among students may also be limited. In addition to the prevailing classroom and school conditions, students' backgrounds are also a major factor in the influence of the hidden curriculum. Age, gender, race, ethnicity, socioeconomic status, disability status, and the linguistic background of students are also determinants of how students will view the world. Disadvantaged students may never be able to develop a personal sense of efficacy related to their local and world environments.

Cultural minority groups that have perennially been discriminated against may find it difficult to believe that the Universal Declaration of Human Rights should be applicable to all peoples of the world; their experience contradicts that. Children of newly arrived immigrants from developing countries would have great difficulty reconciling statements in the U.S. Constitution and the Universal Declaration of Human Rights with the denial to their families of state benefits such as health care, unemployment compensation, and social security. "Life, liberty and the pursuit of happiness" cannot occur if people are not given the freedom and opportunity to do so by their government and, generally, by their social environment. Given this condition, the task of the teacher who is dedicated to providing instruction in global education is enormous. The teacher, operating within the framework of the formal curriculum, must examine the hidden curriculum of the school and his or her classroom. Unless the teacher addresses the consequences of the hidden curriculum on learning and instruction, the aims of global education are not likely to be attained.

WHAT TYPES OF INSTRUCTIONAL STRATEGIES ARE CONSISTENT WITH GLOBAL EDUCATION?

Throughout this text we have argued that problem solving and inquiry type instructional methods are the most appropriate for global studies. This instructional method assumes that learning takes place when the students themselves learn to identify global issues and examine them critically. In this process, students learn how to develop hypotheses about their sociopolitical environment, how to collect relevant data, and how to use the data to confirm or reject their hypotheses. Students also learn how to deal with controversial world issues (i.e., how to analyze a world problem reflectively, how to take a defensible position on the issue, how to make proposals for problem resolution, and how to trace the consequences of their acting on their proposals).

In addition to seeking to understand the world around them and forming empathetic feelings toward their fellow world citizens, teachers need to prompt students to engage in social participation. The type of instructional method needed is one that encourages students to develop strategies for reaching important decision makers. A letter to a leading newspaper editorial section might be one result of this classroom approach. Contacting influential leaders in world organizations might be another outcome of such instruction. As they proceed to act out their reasoned proposals, students learn how to develop action strategies (i.e., how to organize, how to mobilize support for their proposals, how to negotiate and compromise, and how to ensure that mutually agreed decisions were carried out). In this text we have presented some examples of how a simple springboard from a newspaper can be used as a lesson to generate bona fide student activity in all three domains: the cognitive, the affective, and the participatory. Inquiry must begin, however, with divergent rather than convergent types of questions.

Questions that promote divergent thinking generally ask students to relate things in their environment: What is the relationship between armaments and war, especially in neighboring countries? What is the relationship between high tariffs and consumer satisfaction? What are the effects on industrial development of reducing oil production in the Middle East? All of these questions likely generate divergent thinking, which is thinking that opens new horizons for students.

Questions that encourage convergent thinking are those questions that have only one answer: What is the poorest country in South America? What is the GNP of the countries belonging to the NATO alliance? How many miles off a country's coastline are recognized by the world governments as being part of a country's territorial waters? While we recognize that teachers often need to ask some of the latter type of questions, these questions should never be the focal points of classroom discussion. Inquiry teaching and learning is based on the idea that questions should open rather than close thinking and discussion. Questions that anticipate a single answer are inimical to critical thinking and reflection. This is the reason why we have provided inquiry type questions in most of our exercises and examples.

WHAT ARE THE KEY CONCEPTS AND ISSUES FOR GLOBAL EDUCATION?

We expect that while the issues in this book will spark readers' interest, they will not provide adequately for all the material needed for inquiry based instruction in the classroom. We began the in-

depth global issues discussion with consideration of three related topics: human rights, population, and refugees. It is true that human
rights are discussed in U.S. classrooms, usually in connection with discussions of the U.S. Constitution, and usually with the first ten
amendments to the Constitution, known as the "Bill of Rights."
When teachers open up discussion on students rights, they deal directly with universal human rights. Students, like adults, have rights,
and it is the teacher's responsibility to examine all people's rights in
class discussions. However, it is rare to focus on worldwide human
rights. Why were the human rights of several ethnic groups violated
in occupied Europe under Nazi Germany? Why were the rights of the
Armenians violated in Turkey in the beginning of the twentieth century? Why are the human rights of the Kurds and other religious and
ethnic minorities currently being violated by Iraq, Syria, and Turkey?
As they engage in discussions of such cases, students are given the
opportunity to collect materials that relate directly to the issues. The
Universal Declaration of Human Rights should be the first document
students gain access to. Then there are different international organizations that provide information about where these rights are violated (for example, Amnesty International and the International
Court of Justice in the Hague). Are the rights of certain people in different parts of the world violated? Why? Do gender, ethnicity, race,
religion, age, linguistic background, and condition of disability have
something to do with these violations?

The human rights of people are often violated as a result of population changes on a global basis. Many of these changes are forced,
usually for economic or political reasons. Countries with rapidly expanding populations are faced with enormous difficulties in providing adequately for their citizens. The mass exodus of individuals
from Haiti in 1994 clearly demonstrates the predicament of people
in certain countries, forced to flee by any means. Occupying forces,
such as the Turkish forces invading northern Cyprus in 1964, also
forcefully displace certain ethnic groups from their land. When people are forced to leave their country or their land, they become refugees in another country or land. How are they treated in the
country that receives them? Often they are mistreated and suffer as
a result. In this text, we provided examples of where this situation
prevails. How will students in a global education class react to these
events? How should they? Can they develop action plans to offer

input to the important world decision makers? If the students choose to do something about a situation in which the human rights of refugees are being violated, how would they mobilize worldwide support for their endeavor?

Another set of issues discussed in the text concerned the global environment, energy, health, and nutrition. For example, why are about 200 elephants killed every day? Why are vast areas of rainforests in Brazil destroyed every year? What are the consequences of such catastrophic events in the bioenvironment on the people of these lands? What are the implications for the entire world population?

Topics that concern many individuals are how energy is secured from the environment and also the consequences of environmental pollution. The uncontrolled burning of fossils fuels contributes to global warming, an environmental condition that may have devastating implications for the survival of human populations. What can the average citizen do, operating as an individual or member of a group, to prevent or slow down the ill effects of uncontrolled energy consumption? How can people influence world leaders to subscribe to policies that respect the world's bioenvironment? How can the memory of Chernobyl be used as an example of human disregard of the possible effects of processing atomic energy? In the latter case, students can examine the literature that describes the dangerous conditions of the atomic energy plant in Chernobyl, caused by damage in its processing machinery. This accident affected the entire population in the region and people on other continents. Thousands of people died as a result, and as many or more were incapacitated for life.

Related to the study of the environment, we discussed issues of health and nutrition. How can people, especially in the developing world, secure adequate food to sustain themselves? How can they secure potable water? How can they prevent the devastating effects of contagious diseases? These are some of the questions raised in this chapter, with helpful suggestions to the teacher for promoting critical thinking on the issues. The point to remember, however, is that when the issue has been examined critically, action should follow. Awareness by itself will not help resolve local and world problems. Individual or group action is necessary.

Global economics was another topic discussed at length in the text. This topic, much like the other topics presented for discussion in the book, relates to the effects that national or regional systems have on the world. Whether a country chooses to have a socialist or a capitalist economic system, the malfunctioning of the system could affect all other systems in the world. If labor is cheap in one country, how will it affect the prices of goods and services in the rest of the world? What about in countries where labor is expensive? What about in countries where the natural resources for the production of certain goods are not readily available? Does the principle of supply and demand always apply to the production and distribution of goods and services worldwide? Do students agree with some economists who argue that the modern world economy is capitalistic?

World trade is one of the topics that highly concerns students. The clothes students wear, the foods they eat, the cars their parents drive, and the entertainment they experience are all determined by the trade conditions of the world. If relatively high tariffs are imposed by one country on goods manufactured in another, these more expensive goods are not very likely to be bought by the consumers. For example, if the government of the United States, under the instigation of local manufacturers, raised the duties on automobiles imported from Germany, then consumers might buy fewer German automoblies. Countries enter trade associations (for example, the European Union) to safeguard their trade interests. As a result, countries that are members of the European Union are not likely to encourage the importation of automobiles from the United States because the United States is not a member country. It is unfortunate that, despite efforts by world bodies such as the UN and its affiliates, economic competition, rather than cooperation, still prevails among most of the countries in the world. This is especially true in countries that are post-industrial leaders, such as most of the European and North American countries. Here we have a discrepancy—the UN and other international organizations advocate cooperation among nations but trade blocks and regional alliances advocate competition. How can we reconcile these two, seemingly incompatible, demands? What is the role of the average citizen in this?

Global security is another topic that should concern all citizens, because an incident in one country could have immediate repercussions in another country or in the entire world. Iraq, after the unsuccessful invasion of Kuwait in 1990, was prevented from developing weapons of mass destruction. Events in 1997 and 1998 again prompted a confrontation between Iraq and the UN. This was a clear example of UN involvement in global security. Curtailment of terrorist activities, such as when a bomb was exploded in the World Trade Center in New York by terrorists, has been another area in which international cooperation has been sought. Airport security enforced worldwide is one of the means for limiting terrorist activities. Students have reason to learn about terrorism, because the phenomenon is not only observed in the outside world; violent acts can occur in their neighborhoods as well as in school. School security should be associated with global security. Students need to learn how to provide their input in decision making on security, for these are decisions that affect them as well as the well-being of people anywhere in the world. Security considerations, however, shouldn't compromise individual rights.

WHAT ASSESSMENT PROCEDURES REFLECT THE GOALS OF GLOBAL EDUCATION?

Students in global education classes should seek to accomplish the following general goals:

1. The ability to deal with concepts and theories that try to explain how the world system of human interactions works.
2. The development of a global consciousness, a consciousness that gives individuals a sense that they are members of a world community.
3. The predisposition to help the world's environment and a willingness to act in order to bring about justifiable changes in the environment.

Classroom assessment provides the means to ascertain whether educational objectives have been attained. The assessment examples provided in the text were prepared in the spirit of formative rather than summative evaluation. Formative or process evaluation provides feedback to all classroom participants—students, teachers, aides, librarians, administrators, parents, other school associates—regarding their strengths and weaknesses. This type of evaluation does not seek to punish anyone but to identify areas in which instruction may need some change.

In this spirit, we constructed a series of sample instruments that seek to assess global education learning in three domains of classroom activity: the cognitive, the affective, and the participatory.

In the cognitive domain, we emphasized the skills needed to engage students in critical thinking about the world. The ability to develop relational statements explaining global phenomena and to ground these statements with reasons and reliable evidence was the key consideration here. Sample paper-and-pencil assessment items were constructed to match many of the objectives presented in the table of specifications in Chapter 2.

Regarding the affective domain, we provided an example of a controversial article and then followed it with questions seeking to have students identify issues, probe assumptions, develop positions, and detail consequences of acting on their positions. The sample exercises presented in this section sought to clarify—not impose—feelings, attitudes, and values about the global environment.

In the participatory domain we began with a controversial article on religious persecution worldwide and followed it with questions that sought to establish whether students have learned how to contribute to the decisions that affect major world events. Given a reasoned plan of action, do students have the ability to organize and carry through their plans? Have the strategies employed by them gotten results? Should these strategies be revised?

While paper-and-pencil tests provide a measure of what is learned and what needs to be learned by all concerned, they do not provide an authentic picture of the potential that students have in exploring issues concerning the global society. For this reason, we have provided examples of what is known as alternative assessment. This type of assessment consists of informal observations, anecdotal records, rating scales, projects, journals, and portfolios. Examples of these types of informal assessment were provided, stressing global referents in all three domains of knowledge and action. Teachers need to decide for themselves which types of assessment instruments are appropriate for their students (i.e., instruments that would give all concerned a true picture of what is happening in the classroom in their quest to introduce and implement a global perspective).

As schools enter a new century and a new millennium, global education provides a unique opportunity for students and school personnel to look into the future rather than the past. Looking into the future means, in part, that there is a new conceptualization of the role of the individual vis-à-vis the world. While in the past the world was looked at as something distant, the world is now part of the individual's immediate environment. Modern technology helped make this a reality. World issues now become local issues, and unless the individual is prepared to reflect on these issues and take appropriate action, the individual's capabilities cannot meet the demands of the new millennium. The demands of the new millennium include the ability of individuals to deal with an increasing number of alternatives, some of them equally good or bad. The ability to resolve conflict is a pressing demand of the years ahead. Students, in order to meet this demand, need to develop a multilevel understanding (i.e., understanding that social, political, economic, and ecological conflict has many levels, from local to international). The seemingly local conflict or problem, in most cases, has an international or global dimension. The crowding of cities, homeless people, abused children, and sanitation problems are a few of the problems faced by communities worldwide. This phenomenon, emerging as the new millennium is approaching, can be termed "the internationalization of localism." This trend, as one author puts it, is

> a process of institutionalization, in which there is a global creation of locality. This takes several forms. It can be weak institutionalization, in which similar processes of localization are taking place universally, without an overall guiding formal body. Examples of this are the establishment of great numbers of nationalisms with similar characteristics, or the worldwide spread of suburbanization. Alternatively, the creation of locality guided by formal international institutions, such as the International Youth Hostel Association promoting "particularistic" back-to-nature type communalism on a world scale. Other examples are the Pan-African movement: or the Global Forum meeting in Brazil in 1992 to organize globally the promotion of values and identities of native peoples. In each case... there is the "global institutionalization of the expectation and construction of local particularism." (Featherstone & Lash, 1995, pp. 4–5)

Global education provides a road to Ithaca. Will teachers and their students take it?

QUESTIONS FOR REFLECTION

1. How can the systematic introduction of global education into the school curriculum help students meet the promises and challenges of the twenty-first century? What are the most significant promises and challenges of the new century? Explain.

2. Provide examples of how globalization affects each student in the classroom personally or as a member of a local community, state, or nation.

3. Assuming you were given a free hand to construct an "infusion curriculum" for global education, how would you go about doing it? What criteria would you use for selecting the content?

4. How would you use a springboard from a textbook, the Internet, a newspaper article, or a UN document to initiate an inquiry type discussion on a global issue? What types of questions would you ask? What role would you perform as a teacher in critically examining the issues?

5. How do you perceive the difference between convergent and divergent thinking about global issues? Give examples of questions that would generate both kinds of thinking.

6. Make an announced visit to different classes of colleagues in your school. What types of questions do other teachers ask of their students? What kind of advice can you offer them, if any?

7. Given the background of your students (for example, ethnic or racial minorities, students with disabilities, students in inclusion classes), what would you select as the most appropriate concepts and issues on global affairs for classroom discussion?

8. Given the list of concepts and issues prepared above, how would you go about developing a statement of objectives followed by an appropriate content and instructional method? What particular skills should your students exemplify during and after such instruction?

9. What assessment procedures do you prefer using in your classroom and why?

10. Assuming you have examined in depth one of the global issues mentioned in the text, develop a set of instruments or procedures which would give you and your students reliable information on the effectiveness of your instruction. Try to develop assessment procedures in all of the domains presented in this text—cognitive, affective, and participatory.

11. You are making a presentation to educators at a state conference on the topic "Global Education: The Road to the New Millennium." What

would you say to them? How would you describe the philosophy of global education and the expected student outcomes?

REFERENCES

Featherstone, M., & Lash, S. (1995). Globalization, modernity, and the spatialization of social theory: An introduction. In M. Featherstone, S. Lash, & R. Robertson (Eds.), *Global modernities* (pp. 1–24). London, England: Sage.

Massialas, B. G. (1996). Criteria for issues-centered content selection. In R. W. Evans & D. W. Saxe (Eds.), *Handbook on teaching social issues, NCSS Bulletin 93* (pp. 44–50). Washington, DC: National Council for the Social Studies.

Index

DATE DUE

APR 0 9 2003			